HOUSES AND PALACES OF
ANDALUSIA

HOUSES AND PALACES OF
ANDALUSIA

PATRICIA ESPINOSA DE LOS MONTEROS
FRANCESCO VENTURI

RIZZOLI
NEW YORK

The author and photographer would like to thank the following for their assistance and hospitality:

Her Majesty the Queen Margarita of Bulgaria; the Duchess of Alba; the Dukes of Almenara Alta; Rafael Atienza Marquis of Salvatierra; Antonio Benitez Villapol; the Duchess of Granada de Ega; the Marquesses of Caltojar; the Marquesses of Cerverales; Fernando Chueca Goitia; the Cruz Conde family; Carmen Damas de la Chica; Bodegas Pedro Domecq; Mr. and Mrs. Domecq Zurita; Mr. and Mrs. Herruzo; Maria Josefa de Ibarra y Mencos; the Count of Lebrija; Jose Luis Medina del Corral and Jose Victor Rodriguez Caro (Victorio y Lucchino); the Duchess of Medina Sidonia; Elena and Cristina Meneses de Orozco; the Marquesses of Mérito; Carlos Mingarro; Alonso Moreno de la Cova; Nina and Enriqueta Moreno de la Cova; Marta Oriol Pastega; the Duchess of Osuna; Manuel Patiño; Natalio Rivas; Guadalupe Romero Lafitte; Manuel Salinas Benjumea; the Counts of Santa Coloma; Magdalena Sanz Magallon Osborne; Tomás and Ignacio Terry; Paloma Urquijo Domecq; Luis Vañó.

And also the following Institutions:

The Asociación de Propietarios de Casas Históricas y Singulares; the Councils of Carmona, Écija and Granada; the Patronato Municipal de Cultura of Palma del Río; the Directors of the Obra Social y Cultural de Caja Sur (Cordoba); the Consejería de Cultura de la Junta de Andalucía and the Dirección General de Bienes Culturales; Hotel Casa de Carmona; Hotel Palacio de la Rambla.

First published in the United States of America by
Rizzoli International Publications, Inc
300 Park Avenue South, New York, NY 10010

First published in Great Britain by CARTAGO, London
An imprint of KEA Publishing Services Ltd., 63 Edith Grove, London SW10 0LB

Text © 1998 Patricia Espinosa de los Monteros
Photographs © 1998 Francesco Venturi/KEA

ISBN 0-8478-2147-1
LC 98-66581

Translated from the Spanish by Caroline Phipps

Designed by Karen Stafford
Edited by Judy Spours
Production by Elizabeth Harcourt
Map by Sarah-Jayne Stafford
Research by Gastón Segura

Colour origination and printing by Amilcare Pizzi, Milan, Italy

Jacket front CASA DE SALINAS, SEVILLE 'L'-shaped entrance typical of the Arab-inspired Andalusian houses, with the main courtyard at the back. The walls are lime-washed in a strong red ochre.

Jacket back QUINTA DE LOS TERRY, PUERTO DE SANTA MARÍA The chapel bell gable, showing the arrangement of glazed ceramic and clay roof tiles

Frontispiece CASA DE MEDINA SIDONIA, SANLÚCAR DE BARRAMEDA The Patio del Picadero, the oldest part of the house, seen from the gallery. Beyond is the Church of the Mercedes.

CONTENTS

FOREWORD

The subject of this book is undoubtedly an ambitious one – a thorough exploration of the great houses of Andalusia. Although it is sometimes said that an image is worth more than a thousand words, here both the illustrations, by the talented photographer Francesco Venturi, and the text are perfectly balanced. Although the photographs beautifully illustrate the most important Andalusian architectural achievements over the centuries, this book is more than just a photo-album. The text, written by Patricia Espinosa de los Monteros, a journalist specializing in the architecture of houses, also describes in fascinating detail the history of manor houses and palaces across the whole of the region.

The book is as rich and varied as its subject, and it evokes the very essence of Andalusia. It takes us from the serene land of Jaén – whose building styles were dictated by its proximity to the influence of Castile and by its harsh climate – to the great Cordoban houses that perfectly combined Castilian design with Moorish traditions. This is seen, above all, in their magnificent landscaped courtyards and gardens, which inherited the Arab art of using water. The book steers us also to Seville, the great metropolis of Andalusia and of Spain itself, the centre of trade with the New World. Many of Seville's houses are the result of a happy synthesis of architectural elements from other parts of Andalusia, a region which has a special place in the history of architecture and in the evolution of ornamental and decorative features.

An attentive look at the photographs and a calm reading of the text of this book strongly communicate the love Andalusians feel for their houses. They have conserved and maintained, with exquisite care, traditions in architecture and decoration that are the fruit of experience accumulated throughout generations, and which are still admired today.

The Duchess of Alba

Opposite A garden of the Palacio de las Dueñas, Seville, with vibrant bouganvillaea covering the façade of the palace.

CASA DE ARCOHERMOSO, PUERTO DE SANTA MARIA The main, landscaped courtyard with a central fountain and arches on two sides. The blind wall is one side of a storehouse.

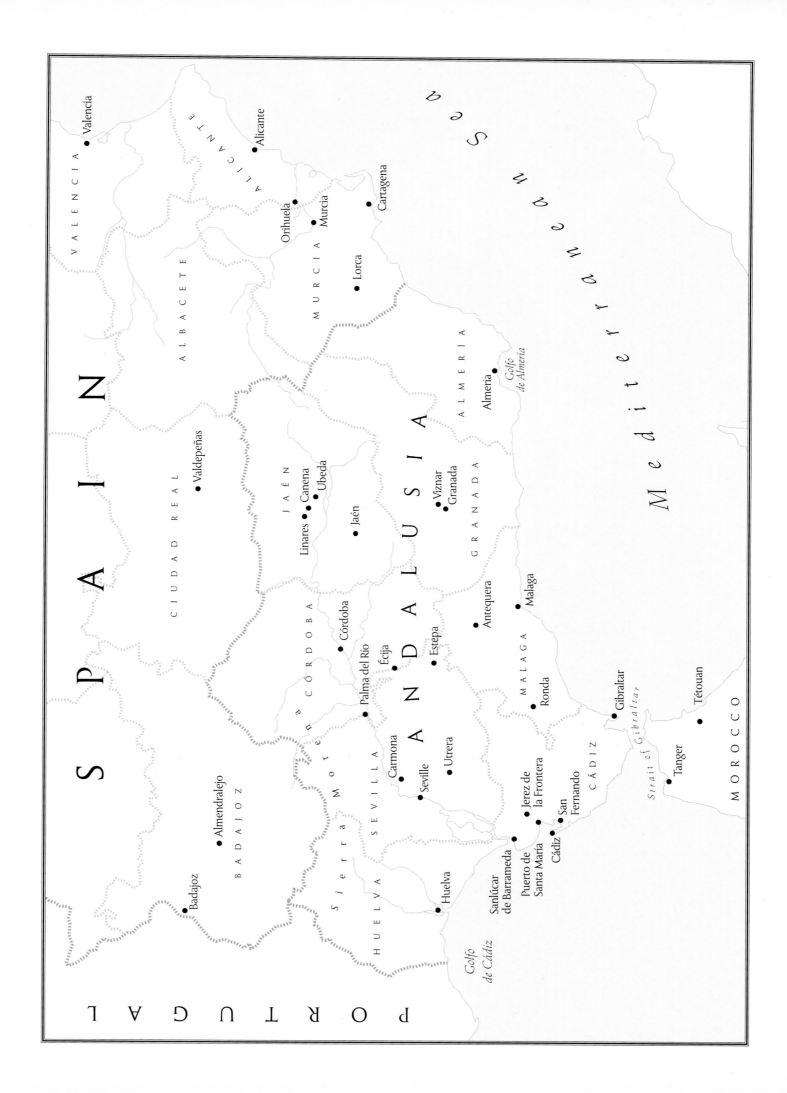

INTRODUCTION

ANDALUSIA IS AN EXTENSIVE REGION formed by eight provinces in the south of the Iberian Peninsula. The great river Guadalquivir, baptized by the Arabs as *el rey* – the king – crosses it from Jaén province to the Atlantic to produce one of the most fertile valleys and most populated marshlands in Spain.

Its climate is both extreme and varied. The Sierra de Grazalema, where rhododendrons and azaleas grow in forests of Spanish fir, has the highest recorded rainfall in Spain. Elsewhere, the peaks of the Veleta in Sierra Nevada are covered with snow all the year round and there are large, almost desert areas in Almería. As a result, the landscapes of Andalusia display all the colours of the rainbow. In the mountains, the white villages stand out against the reddish hillsides; and in the fertile lowlands, in spring, the wheat fields burst out green, speckled with red poppies, and the almond trees flower into snowy blossom. When summer comes to an end, the silver-green of the olive trees rules the countryside; all else has turned to gold, ripened and dried by the implacable sun and heat.

Andalusia faces Africa, which lies only a few miles away from its coasts. It is well protected inland from the plateau of La Mancha and from Castile by the large, rugged mountain chain of Sierra Morena. The name conjures up stagecoach journeys, whose brigands, armed with blunderbusses, literature has taken care to convert into romantic figures – as exotic and slightly fantastic as everything related to this region, but nevertheless part of its history.

Thus, with a little imagination, one can hear distant echoes of men landing on the fine, sandy beaches of Punta de Tarifa and the din of the cruel battles that would change the course of history. Later came the uproar of caravels and schooners setting off for unknown lands, commanded by fearless adventurers,

Page 10 CASA DE OSBORNE, PUERTO DE SANTA MARIA A corner of the well-planted courtyard, which has arches on three sides.

Opposite CASA DE TONI BENITEZ, SEVILLE A view from the house of the courtyards and flat roofs of typical Sevillian baroque houses, with the Giralda in the background.

very often not even seamen. And then, after many decades, the sound of other ships landing along the coasts, loaded with treasures from the other side of the world.

Andalusia's history and influence would be felt throughout Europe. Tartesians, Phoenicians, Carthaginians and Greeks came and left. The Romans settled here, built colonies and villas, developed agriculture and irrigation systems and maintained rich cultural and political centres until they also were ousted by another invasion, this time of the least barbarian of the tribes from the north of Spain.

Andalusia enjoyed a period of stability under the Visigoths, until the first Arab armies arrived in 711, supported by Jews who had been driven out years before and by their Christian leaders, who had secretly summoned them. They remained in the region for no less than eight centuries. Coming from North Africa, from the hot and arid desert, they found in this land the promised paradise of their sacred books. Its gentle climate, fertile soil and warm, welcoming people persuaded them to settle down, intermarry and eventually to establish a rich and

CASTILLO DE CANENA The ground floor entrance to the castle of the town, decorated now with military armour and with hunting trophies.

liberal culture that was completely different from the one that was being created elsewhere in Spain, beyond the mountains bordering Andalusia.

The Arabs built beautiful palaces and magnificent mosques and schools that formed generations of scholars. The study of medicine, in particular, became a priority for the Arabs, who were familiar with the works of Hippocrates and Galen and whose leading figure in this science, the Cordoban Abulcassim El Zaharawi (born in Azahara and physician to Al-Hakam II), enjoyed extraordinary prestige in the medieval Christian world. In addition, in their zeal to find the philosopher's stone, alchemists fostered the Muslim art of refining metals and of dyeing fabrics and leather. The Arabs also reached high levels of knowledge in astrology and philosophy, and in mathematics, including the teaching of algebra, a discipline whose very name is of Arab origin. The Muslims remained in Andalusia until the sixteenth century, when Ferdinand and Isabel drove them out in order to complete the unity of all the regions of the Spanish peninsula.

Pages and pages could be filled with tales and delightful legends about events that took place during the Arab period, such as the stories about Almutamid, Moorish king of Seville. Almutamid was a poet and set up a court of poets and writers. He married a slave named Romaikia, with whom he had

Opposite PALACIO DEL MARQUÉS DEL CARPIO, CORDOBA The vibrant 'Yellow Room' in the tower contains an unusual bureau decorated with the image of the Virgin by the Sevillian sculptor La Roldana (1656-1704), surrounded by scenes of the life of Christ. Against the far wall of the room is an eighteenth-century writing-desk with painted glass panels. *Papier-mâché* chairs match the pedestal- and corner-tables and coordinate with a set of nineteenth-century French chairs, upholstered with the same fabric as the curtains.

PALACIO DE LAS DUEÑAS, SEVILLE The library cum study has a Moorish feel. Italian paintings hang over the tile and brick fireplace in one corner. The carpet and cushions are Moroccan.

PALACIO DE LEBRIJA, SEVILLE The 'Red Room' which leads onto the library. The Aubusson hangings are woven with gold thread.

Opposite PALACIO DE MOLINA DEL POSTIGO, ÚBEDA The sunny, covered loggia of the first floor is simply furnished. The large iron lantern chandelier, reminiscent of Moorish decorative styles, was forged at Úbeda.

fallen hopelessly in love, simply because she had been able to conclude a poem that he had started. They were immensely happy, and one of their daughters would eventually become Queen of Castile. When Almutamid heard that Alfonso VI, King of Castile, was approaching Seville with his hostile armies, he had the brilliant idea of sending the poet Abenamar, his great friend and Court Vizier, to meet him, escorted by a large retinue and loaded with presents. The Visier set up a lavish camp and invited the Castilian King to lunch with him in his tent. When desserts were over, they played a game of chess with additional rules: the loser was to pay the winner an amount of corn. This was calculated by designating two grains to the first square of the board, each number then multiplied by itself until the last square was reached. The King lost the game and realized that he did not have sufficient grain in his whole kingdom to settle the wager. The Vizier generously proposed to forgive the debt in exchange for the withdrawal of his army. And thus it is that a game of chess is said to have saved Seville from a Christian invasion.

The eight centuries of Arab domination were fruitful in many ways. It was a period of interchange, of peaceful cohabitation, of blood unions. There were times when the relationships between Muslim and Christian kings were even based on friendship, mutual loyalty and honour. When the Arabs were forced to leave, they were heartbroken to have to abandon their most valued treasures – the palaces, mosques, gardens and houses that were a private, contained celebration of the senses.

As they gradually conquered the land from the Arabs and became familiar with their customs, habits and organization, the Christian kings made them their own and adopted many Arab traditions and manners quite unlike those practised in other European courts. A travelling chronicler named Rosmital described the customs of the court of Enrique IV as exotic and strange. He tells how they drank, ate and dressed in the Arab fashion and how the King wore a turban and received him sitting on cushions on the floor, with the Queen at his side.

Arab dress and craftsmanship lingered a long time in Christian Andalusia, but it was above all in architecture that the Moorish influence remained strongest. This Andalusian style appears on the region's buildings either in anonymous and unobtrusive ways or, on the contrary, profusely and prodigiously, depending on a thousand unknown circumstances, about which we can only speculate. Its quality may depend on the architect who drew up the plans, on the talents of the ceramists and carpenters to express in their works a beauty that neither time nor passing fashions would destroy, or simply on the whim of a wealthy owner.

After the Christian conquest, many amazing manor houses began to be built in the towns of Andalusia. The Castilian aristocracy now felt secure in the territory and protected from new invasions and gradually abandoned military fortifications and started to build more comfortable and luxurious houses. They were at their most lavish and splendid after the discovery of America and the appointment of Seville as the customs city of the 'New World'. These manor houses, like those raised in Salamanca, Avila, Valladolid, Valencia, Barcelona, Toledo and in all the other Christian cities in the country, had to be worthy reflections of their owners' rank. There were a number of influences on the architecture at this time. For example, the Castilian court greatly admired the flamboyance and cultivation of private luxury displayed in the buildings of the Italian Renaissance nobility. Such a lifestyle was becoming economically feasible in Spain as a result of the riches pouring into Seville from America; it was a constant flow that spread a spirit of cheerful squandering totally unknown until then in Andalusia.

After this period of extravagant building, palaces and manor houses continued to be built over the following two centuries, but they never again achieved the magnificence of the Casa de Pilatos in Seville or of the superb palaces of Úbeda on which they were modelled, and to which the earlier architects and owners conferred a personality of their own. Cryptic Moorish details were still included, but mostly for sentimental reasons. A genuine Andalusian baroque style began to appear, one quite different to the baroque of Bernini's Rome. Spain itself had changed, too; it was still the greatest world Empire yet known, but it was already a wounded one.

The nineteenth century saw the building of few great mansions. Spain was on the brink of the industrial revolution, but the century also saw a Napoleonic occupation and a patriotic war, three civil wars, a Savoyard king, a republic as romantic and short-lived as a summer romance and four constitutions. In short, it was an effervescent century, full of intentions and of military coups, but an uneasy one for capital and for industry.

Nineteenth-century houses were elegant *palacetes* of Spanish Renaissance style mingled with eclectic flavours of Parisian Empire and the subtle decoration of English romanticism. As the century came to an end, manor houses tended to become increasingly more exotic, in a colonial style, and it was fashionable to fill them with motley collections of furniture and treasures. But their architects never managed to create a style of their own as their predecessors had.

The productive wealth of Spain moved to Catalonia, to the Basque country and to Asturias. Andalusia retired back within itself, content with its traditions and ceremonies, attractive and seductive, a continuous source of inspiration for romantic poets, musicians and writers who came here from afar to admire, learn and write – artists and travellers as diverse as Lord Byron, Ravel, Mussorgsky, Rilke, Glinka and Orson Welles.

CARMEN DE LOS MÁRTIRES, GRANADA A detail of the garden, with its towering palm trees and art nouveau fountain.

THE HISTORY OF ARCHITECTURE IN ANDALUSIA

THE ARCHITECTURE OF THE GREAT HOUSES AND PALACES of Andalusia is closely related to the historical events that took place in the region. After the violent period of the *Reconquista*, the Castilian sovereigns – Don Rodrigo, Don Pedro, Doña María, Isabel and Ferdinand, Don Carlos – gradually realized the magnificence of the legacy left behind by the Muslim culture. In triumph or defeat, alone or with their retinue, on horseback or in carriages, they all passed through Andalusia's towns, from Cordoba to Jerez, from Antequera to Sanlúcar. They lived in the Moorish palaces, drank and ate the produce of the land, commanded their armies, were happy or unhappy, wrong or right, and they were the men and women who also contributed towards the making of Andalusia. The noble families – the Guzmáns and the Mendozas and the winemakers of Jerez – left their mark on Andalusian art and architecture by building a hospital or a church, lovely houses or imposing castles.

The Moorish style, its aura and its decoration, nevertheless lingered on for centuries, long after the towns were conquered. The Castilians, Asturians, Leonese and even Basques and Galicians, recently arrived with the troops or labourers, summoned by their lords to repopulate this dazzling and rich new land, perceived the Moorish influence everywhere. It was evident in the newly-built churches, many still facing the *quibla* as the mosques had, in the busy narrow streets, in the red pavings, and in the glazed tile friezes and clay pots the settlers found in their new homes – which, of course, had once been Muslim houses.

Page 22 PALACIO DE VIZNAR

A detail of some of the wonderful fresco scenes derived from the story of Don Quixote on the lower gallery of the palace in the town.

Right   PALACIO DE VIZNAR   A splendid view of the fresco-decorated façade of the palace from the summer garden, with its original myrtle hedges and stone fountains. The gardens still contain their old box hedges, too, and some plant specimens over a hundred years old. The frescos on the lower gallery show scenes from the story of Don Quixote and those on the upper gallery, mythological scenes.

Opposite   PALACIO DE VIZNAR   The façade of the Palace, built by an Italian architect in 1795 as the summer residence of the Archbishop Moscoso.

In these houses, the new artisans learnt the secular skills of the Arab craftsmen. They carefully studied the details of a carved wooden ceiling, of a painted peacock and of the curved pistils on a piece of chipped tilework, or of the fragile arabesques of a broken lattice shutter abandoned in a corner. The Moorish echo is a constant, muted resonance that came to life in the skilled hands and sensitivity of a young Renaissance apprentice studying to become master of his craft. And, curiously, the further the Christian conquest receded in memory and in time, the more marked the arabesques in the tiling and in the coffering became. The

Left PALACIO DE VIZNAR A detail of one of the Don Quixote frescos. The grafitti was inflicted during the Spanish Revolution.

Above PALACIO DE VIZNAR The colours of the frescos are even more satisfying once they have gently faded.

PALACIO DE VIZNAR The impressive stone staircase, decorated with paintings of Italian villas and gardens.

bays of the arches became more loop-shaped, intricate laceries appeared in the wooden ceilings and colourful tiles enlivened loggias or the embrasure of a window. The dazzled owners of the new houses demanded Moorish ornamentation and the craftsmen skilfully complied: Andalusian art started taking shape.

THREE CENTURIES OF WAR

Andalusia did not find peace easily. From the death of Al-Mansur to that of Pedro 'the Cruel', Andalusia suffered three hundred years of disasters and wars and devastating invasions. From the year 1000 onwards, the Caliphate endured assaults, changes of power and movements of frontiers. On the death of Al-Mansur, intermittent Christian raids began, one of the most famous being the ferocious occupation of Cordoba by the Counts of Barcelona and Urgel in 1010. But the valley of the Guadalquivir was not only ravaged from the north; voraciousness soon approached from the south. Greedy for riches and blinded by a fanatical religiousness, tribes of savage Berbers arrived: first the Almoravids (1086), summoned by the Taifa kings of al-Andalus to clear this sweet paradise that Allah had granted his believers in the West of its reprobate governors; and then the Riff Almohads (1170), tired of the bartering between the Almoravids and the Christians.

PALACIO DE LOS CÓRDOVA, GRANADA A view of the garden, with romantically overgrown walls and cypresses.

PALACIO DE LOS CÓRDOVA A bronze bust of Carlos V in the main dining room on the ground floor.

Between them all, they left very little of the legendary Caliphal civilization. It is enough to say that Al-Hakem II's library of 400,000 volumes – the largest compendium of knowledge of his time – burned, day and night, for three weeks on the shores of the Guadalquivir on orders given by the Almohad dauphin Al-Mansur Yacub, with the people rejoicing around the purgative pyre. During these 'purifying' racial invasions, the scholars in Almería fled eastward, the Mozarabs to the valleys of the Duero and to depopulated Aragón, and the Jews to the

Opposite CASA DE LOS CONDES DE CASA GALINDO, SEVILLE The old staircase rises up out of the courtyard.
Below CASA DE LOS CONDES DE CASA GALINDO One of the old annexes of the summer house has been converted into a bohemian apartment by the designer Marta Oriol.

MONASTERIO DE SAN FRANCISCO, PALMA DEL RÍO

One of the courtyards at the entrance to the monastery, brightly limewashed.

Opposite MONASTERIO DE SAN FRANCISCO

The old hospital nave has been converted into a living room and billiards room.

new boroughs along the Santiago Way and La Mancha, or to the more tolerant *taifa* of Murcia.

This was the turbulent scene before the battle of Navas de Tolosa, although it is said that when Sancho VII of Navarre pulled off the chains that protected the *jaima* of Miramamolín, the Almohad empire collapsed, and with it, Muslim dominion. And when Ferdinand II conquered Seville in 1248, only two Islamic realms remained on the peninsula – Granada and Niebla. The latter would not hold out long, however, and in 1261, Alfonso X and the Guzmáns seized it, together with Huelva and the valley of the Guadalquivir. The Nasrids of Granada were quick to acknowledge and renew their subjugation before the Castilian King and remained relatively independent by paying tributes, until they also fell in 1492.

Granada had become an immense workshop producing and distributing artefacts that enjoyed great prestige throughout the Christian West: the gilt pottery of Malaga, the damasks, brocades and fabrics of Malaga and Granada, jewel boxes and popular perfume bottles carved in ivory, as well as fantastic silverwork. All these exquisite pieces were stored in warehouses at the port of Almería to be sent out to markets all over the world. Nothing was lacking in the kingdom of Granada: it received African traders and it had workshops and ports. In addition, its fertile lowlands produced more than enough to sustain the Moors who had settled here in their flight from other areas.

In 1261, with Alfonso X, 'the Wise', on the throne, an event that is relevant to our story occurred: the arrival of the first Genoese, diplomatic and cunning traders who were to be decisive in the future of Castile. The Italians were skilful seamen and had come to Andalusia to help the Castilians land in Morocco. This had been a project of Ferdinand III, 'the Saint', which consisted of establishing Castilian factories, similar to those in Granada, along the African coast. The King wanted to extend his lands to the other side of the straight in order to smother, or at least curb, any new Berber invasion, with the additional advantage of facilitating trade with the camel trains that supplied the kingdom of Granada with slaves, precious woods, gold, gems and perfumes.

His son, Alfonso X, decided to accomplish his father's dream, but only after careful planning. He started by constructing the Ataranzanas, the Seville dockyards and the arsenal fortress of Castile's future Atlantic fleet. Then he summoned the Genoese, expert navigators, to the African coast to help him. Although the project started out with the best of will, the landing at Salé was unsuccessful.

In spite of the failure of the operation, the Genoese did not leave Seville; on the contrary, they settled down there comfortably and firmly. They had a very powerful reason for doing so: they were enemies of the Catalans in the west Mediterranean and Seville offered them a strategic shelter in the Aragonese rearguard. Naturally, the Castilians, who coveted the riches that were out of their reach for lack of navigators experienced in African waters, were quite happy about the Italian settlement. Eventually, with the Italians' help, they reached the coasts of Africa in search of the Sudanese gold route and of the silk and spice routes. But if the advice and guidance of the Genoese were important in the politics of the Castilian admiralty, they were also crucial to the history of manor houses and palaces in Andalusia. A Genoese, Francisco de Pinelo, built the first palace in Seville; thus, it was from Genoa that the magnificent marble used in the Casa de Pilatos came and through Genoa that the Renaissance arrived in Granada.

Another key event in this story took place in 1263, with the Mudéjar revolt in Murcia and in the valley of the Guadalquivir. It had lasting consequences for Spain and Andalusia. The rebels were driven out, and with them went the intensive agriculture of the great fertile lowlands of southern Spain. The Castilians repopulated the land with serfs, but this did not solve the problem. The Moors had formed a community of small landowners who had stabilized the social base of al-Andalus, but the new Andalusia was organized under the large, landed estates in the hands of the new conquerors. The rich and intensive agriculture of the region disappeared for ever.

LORDS AND CASTLES

After conquering Seville and Niebla, the Castilians started building in the regained cities. The architectural style was an incipient and rudimentary Gothic, of

CASA DE VELAZQUEZ, SEVILLE The large basin fountain in the courtyard is typical of such a seventeeth-century Sevillian house.

Opposite CASA DE VELAZQUEZ A detail of a door, showing both the heavy wood structure and one panel of an eighteenth-century painted folding screen beyond.

interest in that it introduced stonework for the first time in the area, where the masons were used to working with clay, brick and plaster.

This Gothic style, named *Alfonsí* after Alfonso X, ruler at the time, appeared in the kingdoms of Jaén, Cordoba and Seville, its grandeur an attempt to emphasize the authority of the conquerors, who built their houses over the top of the Moorish foundations. The resulting buildings were shocking, for neither the forms nor the materials used resembled those of the former Arab constructions. There was Christian stone rather than Moorish brick and high, pointed Gothic arches instead of lower, horseshoe Moorish ones. The buildings were raised in bare, sober stone, contrasting with the brick and mortar, limewash and adobe used in Moorish architecture. The Gothic style was all vaulted ribs, whereas the Arabs coated their walls with hanging decorations, plasterwork, loop-shaped ornaments and decorative tilework. The Mudéjars resented these new styles that destroyed their art and fled to the kingdom of Granada, leaving behind the grey stone and Christian gloom.

Who was then left to carry on the building crafts? The Arab stonemasons and master-builders – the *alarifes* – had gone, but their art remained in countless details that would seep into the styles deployed by new generations of craftsmen. In this way, the Moorish style was revived, in the masonry, in the *artesonados*, in the interlaced decorations of the manor houses.

Meanwhile, the military orders and the aristocracy retreated to their castles and fortresses, faced with the repeated threat of attacks from Moroccan Arabs. These new lords, like the Almohads before them in the government of the Guadalquivir, were not interested in luxury palaces or in poetry, but only in fighting and in living in the strictest military austerity. A good example of their ilk are the Guzmáns, the most powerful family of the reign of Seville, who kept their dark, damp and uncomfortable fortress of Niebla for over a century. Military requirements – the lord of Sanlúcar held the title of Protector of the Atlantic Fleet – obliged them to move to their palace at Sanlúcar de Barrameda near the mouth of the river Guadalquivir. Only after they had settled there did they remodel the place, also built on the remains of an Arab citadel, and provided it at last with some comforts.

The majority of Castilian noblemen acted under this same itinerant and provisional warrior spirit, and a town house was unthinkable during these years. Even a fixed residence seemed inappropriate for feudal lords, the owners of extensive properties, received from royal grants in the new Andalusian kingdoms, that required their constant presence and attention. Thus, civil Castilian building was limited to reinforcing barbicans and the towers of the existing castles; more than that, even the construction of new small forts was inconceivable. The King was an exception. At that time he commissioned two buildings in Seville: the Atarazanas and the tower-house of Don Fadrique. But Don Alfonso still identified with the prevailing spirit and both buildings were put to military use. The Atarazanas of Seville were the King's most ambitious construction, designed as dockyard and arsenal for Castile's expeditionary fleet to the Indies and to Africa. They were a vast undertaking, although nothing has remained of them.

The Torre de Don Fadrique is the only Alfonsine building that remains standing in Seville, in Santa Clara street. The stark square tower, popularly known as *Torre Mocha* (blunt tower), was named after its designer, the King's brother, the Infante Don Fadrique. Within its boundaries, the Infante and the very young widow of his father, King Ferdinand III, lived their sad story of forbidden love. There they went to hunt and walk far from the accusing eyes of a court that condemned their relationship. The tower is the remains of an intended military fort, but the singular elegance of the building and its perfectly polygonal floor-plan suggest the luxury of a residential building that must surely have adjoined it. Perhaps it had been the Christians' first attempt to raise a palace in the conquered Andalusia. Whatever the case, we know little more of this castle, watch-tower or retreat, and all we can do now is admire it.

CASA DE FERNANDO CHUECA, SEVILLE A house in the Santa Cruz district has a typical baroque staircase skirted with Moorish blue and white tiles. A painting of Saints Justa and Rufina, patrons of the city, hangs on the wall.

THE KING'S PALACES

King Pedro I of Castile was an important figure in the world of art and architecture. He emerged as a man in advance of his time, a controversial and forceful character, nicknamed by some *el Justiciero* (the Just) and by others 'the Cruel'. He reigned during a challenging time and had to cope with complicated state matters and attacks from the nobility as well as with his own very serious family problems. He did his best to appease his half-brothers of the Guzmán family, but they spurned his efforts.

He was a passionate man, much loved and much hated. It is said that he ordered one of his half-brothers to be executed, that he imprisoned many noble rebels, that he fought duels and that he forced the court to acknowledge his mistress as his legitimate wife and Queen of Castile. But it is also said that he loved the Arab and Hebrew cultures and used them against the self-serving obfuscation of the bishops, and that he was murdered, very young, in the Campos de Montiel by Beltrán Duguesclin and his half-brother, the future Enrique II, *El de las Mercedes*.

King Pedro was a devotee of architecture and lived in and rebuilt the most beautiful houses of his kingdoms. In Andalusia, he embellished the castles of Almodovar and Carmona and restructured the Reales Alcázares of Seville, former palace of Almutamid. All these buildings later became important models for Renaissance architecture.

The Alcázares were enhanced at that time with the elegant decoration we see today: the Mozarab cornices on the façade and the reaches of the superimposed and crossed arches on columns and the main courtyard, known as the Patio de las Doncellas. But what really amazed the people at the time was the great throne room, known as the Ambassadors' Hall, which was covered by a semi-spherical framework that is one of the most beautiful ornamental works in Spain. The King summoned the best Arab master-builders from Granada to work on it for many years. With Pedro, the Moorish style, the *Andalusí*, had returned to Seville. A hundred and fifty years later, when Pinelo designed his house and the Enríquezes started building the Casa de Pilatos and the Palacio de las Dueñas, they were influenced by the grandeur of these castles. Without them, and without the dazzling achievement of the Alhambra in Granada, the magnificent Sevillian residences would not be what they are today.

TIMES OF CHANGE

During the fourteenth century, Spain suffered its first great famine (1320) and Castile was shaken by three catastrophic outbreaks of the Black Death. The epidemic reached such proportions that even the royal palaces were affected and it reduced the population by more than a third. To make matters worse, a civil war broke out. The small towns suffered these disasters most, due to their dependency on the devastated Castilian countryside for food. But winds of change started to blow and new lights began to appear on the horizon. Paradoxically, the Castilian nobility came out of these continuous misfortunes extraordinarily strengthened.

No more than a dozen families (the Mendozas, the Guzmáns, the Zúñigas, the Pachecos, the de la Cuevas, the Enríquez, the Pimentels, the Velascos, the Lunas and the Fajardos) divided the kingdom up into zones of undisputed hegemony that not even the monarch could challenge. They dominated the *Consejo de la Mesta*, the alliance of cattle breeders, and, as a result, the Cantabrian ports and the Flemish factories. They imposed their will on the King of Castile, participated in the succession to the Portuguese throne and included in their ranks the newly-established lineage of the Trastamara family from Antequera, who ruled over Aragón. In spite of its strength, this omnipotent aristocracy resisted settling in the cities. Its way of thinking and of exercising power still depended too much on armed force for it to abandon its military forts. The aristocracy's forays in support of a king or of a pretender to a throne kept the three crown kingdoms up in arms, and Castile lived in conditions of permanent civil war. This state of affairs continued until the arrival of Ferdinand and Isabel and their strong, authoritarian government.

The aristocracy did not, then, start building large palaces or town houses until around 1490. Before they could be persuaded to move to the cities, three conditions needed to be in place: the forced pacification of the territory by an absolute and powerful monarch in the form of Isabel of Castile; a change to a mentality which could entertain the Renaissance; and an armed undertaking common to the whole kingdom, first the conquest of Granada and, then, of America.

THE RENAISSANCE

THE NEW ITALIAN ARCHITECTURAL STYLES took Europe by storm. In Spain, as elsewhere, architects hastened to apply the classical spirit and orders that inspired these perfect, pure forms to their own buildings, while at the same time imposing extra refinements in order to better reflect the prestige of the owners of the houses. The great Andalusian mansions of the sixteenth century, like almost all European manor houses, were the fruit of this new, classical style which constituted modern, Renaissance design.

The Andalusian manor houses developed their own, particular style that was much admired and which inspired architects for at least three centuries. As we have seen, however, the construction of palaces did not start until the aristocracy felt the need to settle nearer, or within, the cities, which did not happen until well into the fifteenth century. The first of the new Castilian city noblemen then started building their houses in the fertile valley of the river Guadalquivir.

These Renaissance mansions were, in fact, designed on the basis of two premises: the functional and the symbolic. They read like books about the status of their inhabitants. The classical symbolism they used was set out in such works as *Laberinto de Fortuna* by Juan de Mena. Later writers like Jorge de Montemayor, Cristóbal de Villaton and Francisco Colonna translated the motifs to read as an allegory to be used in architecture. These authors created a code by which the noblemen could clearly state his position in court, his ambitions and his prestige through the decoration and layout of his residence. This ornamental language was assimilated to such an extent by the Castilian aristocracy that it was even included in the design of their tombs. Classical themes such as Virtue, Love, Fame, Fortune or Wisdom, usually described in literary allegories, also had specific architectural representations: the arrangement of elements on

PALACIO DE LAS DUEÑAS, SEVILLE
A corner of the main courtyard exhibits a
number of the different crafts used in the
construction of the palace: woodwork,
plasterwork, ironwork, tiling and stonework.

a façade or the design of gardens, for example. The placing of some rooms in relation to others or the choice of decorative materials were not a matter of mere inspiration, but rather of a precise architectural language, talking subtly and eloquently of social standing.

Accordingly, the Casa de Pilatos symbolized the classical Temple of Fame and the Casa de las Dueñas the Temple of Love. In the latter, a motif of sylvan figures holding a coat-of-arms represents the forces of nature that protect and keep guard over the household's noble lineage. This singular use of the metaphor is apparent in the choice, apparently loaded with meaning, of these caryatids rather than of representations of Hercules to support an entablature. The presence inside medallions of such figures as grotesques, or their use as columns, is not, then, a result of free inspiration on the part of the stonemason. On the contrary, his designs were based on those allegoric items that best represented the ambitions of the mansion's owner. And so the houses contained, like the chapters of a book, allegorical and mysterious dispositions that only the initiated would know how to interpret. Such magnificence, such display of knowledge and such architectural sensuality reached a climax during the sixteenth century, the height of the Spanish Renaissance and the richest period for our manor houses.

THE CITIES

During this period, the cities became the satellites of the kingdom. Ferdinand and Isabel encouraged the aristocrats to abandon their medieval castles and to settle in the cities. Few of these nobles were now able to keep their feudal privileges, precisely because the monarchs did their best to weaken them. Fortifications were removed from the top of towers and their construction even became forbidden, so that the barons and their families moved to the towns that offered greater security and comfort.

Some of the sovereigns' political actions directly affected architecture and town life. The expulsion of the Jews, for example, which emptied Spain of its secular middle class, would eventually have irreversible effects on the country's financial system and on its sciences. This eviction also allowed the houses in the Jewish quarters, the *aljimas*, to be auctioned at low prices, which resulted in habitable areas within the city walls becoming available to the large number of labourers pouring in from the country. There, they were being pressured by the Mesta, whose abuse of their privileges resulted in their impoverishment.

The cities gradually took shape, with the trade associations and guilds as the backbone of civic life: the guild masters, foremen and apprentices constituted the majority of the urban population. Each guild had its own magistrates, archives and statutes granted by the King and each built a chapel to celebrate its patron saint. All this produced a new and busy urban life in which the King's officials and craftsmen formed the main nucleus, but which also included innumerable beggars and an emerging small aristocracy. This was made up of enriched

Opposite CASA DE SALINAS, SEVILLE The
'L'-shaped entrance is typical of the Arab-
inspired Andalusian houses. The main
courtyard is seen beyond. The walls are
limewashed in a strong red ochre.

craftsmen, wealthy converts and second sons of the Spanish grandees, a social group which started to enlarge its residences in a desire to display suitable grandeur. The aristocracy were careful to make sure that their houses were not too similar to the grand military fortresses of the very powerful, but by using Renaissance symbolism they found the appropriate language with which to adorn their mansions.

In the meantime, the idle noblemen, with no battles to fight, were, as we have seen, slowly attracted by this busy urban life. Every time a grandee decided to settle in one of the towns of his dominions, he would raise a mansion displaying the full force of his power, and the Renaissance palace was born.

INTERIORS

With a little imagination, we can conjure up domestic scenes from the past – the bustle of a kitchen, a ball held in a hall richly decorated with tapestries and hangings, or a morning walk in a garden. The large Andalusian Renaissance houses are no exception. The design of the houses was based first on the practicalities seen in the local, vernacular architecture. The houses of the south were intelligently designed to protect their inhabitants against the heat. In the city, these considerations are apparent in the difference between the summer and winter quarters, for example, or in the loggias and corridors through which the air could circulate freely. To cope with the climate, the houses had small windows opening onto the street, clay floors, tiled panels, esparto mats and quiet, shady courtyards and gardens. All these elements are still used today in modern, southern Spanish houses based on traditional designs.

This classical Andalusian house, with its all important *patio*, or courtyard appeared first in the fifteenth century, inspired by the Greek and Roman houses that the Arabs had used as models, adding their own particular decoration. Although

CASA DE SALINAS A detail of the skirting of glazed Sevillian tiles with stylized floral motifs which is seen in many parts of the house.

Opposite CASA DE SALINAS A view of the main courtyard shows the splendidly carved arches of both loggias.

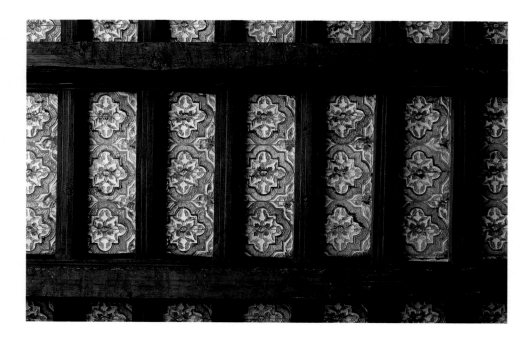

CASA DE SALINAS A detail of the wooden ceiling, inset with glazed ceramic tiles, in the 'L'-shaped entrance.

CASA DE SALINAS A view of the upper terrace, with its stone balustrade and lovely, decorative tiling.

Opposite CASA DE SALINAS The gallery on the upper floor around the main courtyard is glazed in with stained glass.

CASA DE SALINAS A lower room was once part of the summer living-quarters of the palace, situated between two courtyards and lined with windows and mullions to facilitate cooling breezes. The tiles on the floor and walls date from the nineteenth century.

CASA DE SALINAS A tracery window recess in a room on the lower floor.

CASA DE SALINAS Stained glass made in the factory of La Cartuja, signed by its designer R. Escribano.

PALACIO DE LAS DUEÑAS Access to the ballroom is through one side of the main courtyard. The wooden ceilings and frieze carvings are elaborate and the tiled floor is covered with Andalusian mats and copper braziers. On either side of the central glass chandelier hang two oil lamps. In the centre of the room, on a wood and bronze pedestal, is a statue of the famous flamenco dancer La Macarrona, by the sculptor Mariano Benlliure. On either side are French armchairs upholstered in red velvet and on the walls are two large seventeenth-century Brussels tapestries, signed by Van der Hecke.

CASA DE MEDINA SIDONIA, SANLÚCAR DE BARRAMEDA In the 'Column Room', a large eighteenth-century *jardinière* from Talavera, near Madrid, rests on a seventeenth-century pedestal decorated with the crests of the Church of Mercedes. The sixteenth-century Italian hangings either side are woven with the coats-of-arms of the Montalto, the Italian branch of the Dukes' line. Below them is a pair of Renaissance coffers.

each Andalusian town developed its individual style, the general appearance and certain fundamental elements of these houses were very similar wherever they were built. The façades were limewashed and formed a blind wall on the outside, sometimes with a white-painted plinth. The doors were decorated with knockers or with mullioned windows and maintained the Arab custom of being kept closed - until the Inquisition of 1478 ordered them to be kept open all day long so that the Holy Office could publicly check that no offences to the Faith were being committed in the privacy of the home. This change of habits provoked the design of incredibly intricate, grilled front doors and of the *casapuertas*, porches or entrance areas, that appeared later, during the baroque period.

The arrangement of the main areas of a house varied from town to town, but the front entrance generally opened onto a *zaguán*, or lobby, that sometimes included an *apeadero*, an area for carriages and horses. The courtyard was approached through an elbow-shaped passage that made it invisible from the outside, either to preserve the intimacy of the home or for defensive reasons. The street door and the courtyard door rarely faced each other at this time. Later, the Christian mansions were designed with courtyards that could be seen from the main entrances, but by then they were protected by iron lattice gates.

The life of the house was centred around the courtyard, which was decorated with stone or marble columns, tiled panels and plaster friezes. Loggias ran along the ground and first floors, corresponding to the typical division of Andalusian houses into two separate living-quarters. The ground floor was used in the summer to take advantage of the gardens, fountains, courtyards, breezes and shade, and in winter the household moved upstairs, where it was less damp and where the rooms were furnished with carpets, tapestries, fireplaces or braziers.

Staircases also varied in design, but during the Renaissance they generally rose from one side of the courtyard. In the sixteenth century, stairs became grander and they were often cloistered. The stair openings and ceilings were usually very ornate, often coffered and decorated with tiled panels and plasterwork friezes. The flat roofs, or *azoteas*, were bordered by Arab-style balconies and loggias used for sitting or strolling in the fresh air. These galleries, or promenades, were later enclosed and were of monumental proportions in the Renaissance palaces.

The *salas*, or living rooms, were generally arranged around the loggias on both floors and were interconnected. Each room had several functions and was sometimes named after its use (the Queen's Dressing Room, the Ladies' Chamber, the Marquis' Chamber). In other cases, the name was more ambiguous: Hall of the Panelled Fireplace, the Rich Room and so on. The layout and division of the different rooms, or even of different parts of the same room, was often managed with tapestries and draperies. The drape-master was often a permanent member of the household and was also in charge of setting up dining tables and *estrados* in the various rooms.

Spanish houses typically contained one or more *estrado*. The medieval and Renaissance *estrado* consisted of a wooden platform adorned with rich carpets and tapestries, drapes and cushions, where the masters of the house received their visitors, sitting on the floor beside low tables. Later on, the function of the *estrado* changed and it was only used by the ladies, while the gentlemen sat on low stools at their feet. Silver boxes filled with orange or jasmine blossoms placed on low tables or on small writing-desks perfumed the rooms.

There were no dining rooms as such: meals were served on tables made of folding planks which were set up in any room. If the monarchs were invited to a large banquet, a canopied platform would be installed for them and an uncovered one for the rest of the guests. The gold and silver table services were placed on separate tables. The tableware, and the dishes offered, were a sign of the hosts' refinement. Often during the meals, tales of battles or courtly poems would be declaimed and even musicians were sometimes hired to enliven the celebration.

Sleeping-quarters included a chamber, master bedroom and toilet room. The chamber and the bedroom were windowless and opened onto a small reception room. The toilet room contained everything a nobleman might require, from night clothes and an armchair, with its hidden chamber pot, to prayer books and strong-boxes.

The floors were laid with baked clay tiles which were watered in summer against the heat. They could be of different shapes and were usually combined with ceramic strips or wedges called *olambrillas*. Later, the Italian influence meant that marble tiles were brought from Genoa or Carrara. The floors of the living rooms were embellished with Turkish or oriental carpets and rugs.

The walls were covered with panels of abstract patterned tiles, although the blue and white Talavera tiles that appeared in the sixteenth century were painted with naturalistic flowers or animals. The remaining wall surface was limewashed, burnished and hung with rich fabrics and tapestries, gold-edged damasks and embossed leather, an indication of the Arab heritage that still pervaded the interior decoration of the houses. In summer, the tapestries and draperies were changed for lighter materials and mats were spread on the floor and hung over the skirting to refresh the atmosphere.

The pictures on the walls of the noblemen's houses during the sixteenth century were Italian or Flemish paintings on board depicting religious subjects, to which mythological themes and still-lifes were timidly added in the seventeenth century.

The coffered wooden ceilings, the *artesonados*, were extremely rich and sometimes included carved figures or decorative paintings. There were various types of *artesonados:* Mudéjar lacery with a wooden frieze (*arrocabe*), slanted panels (*faldetas*) and horizontal central panels (*almizate*). The stalactite ceilings were usually polychrome and the caissoned ceilings (*casetones*) had criss-crossed beams forming geometrical patterns. A curious custom developed of hanging objects from the beams of these ceilings in the sitting rooms. Copper discs made lovely sounds when moved by the breeze, or pieces of coloured glass created attractive patterns of multi-coloured light.

In the Muslim palaces, baths were particularly important and housed in separate pavilions with stuccoed walls and vaults. The building contained a dressing room, a room for hot baths and another for cold baths, as well as a complicated system for heating the air and letting out the steam.

The gardens of the Mudéjar palaces were designed to stimulate the senses by creating arrangements agreeable to sight, hearing, touch, taste and smell. The water, flowers, combinations of light and shadow and fruit trees all existed for this purpose in small paradises designed for enjoyment. Books and chronicles describe the legendary beauty of the gardens of the palace of Alamiriya and of Medina Azahara in Cordoba, those of the Alhambra or the Generalife in Granada, and the loveliness and sensuality of the gardens of the Crucero del Alcázar in Seville. The architects of the Renaissance palaces of Andalusia fell under the enchantment of their Arab predecessors and continued including pools, fountains, spouts, flowerbeds and aromatic plants in their gardens. The paths may now be paved with brick, painted white or lined in concrete, but they all still lead to the real nucleus or centre of the garden, the courtyard. In the design of almost all these houses, a courtyard surrounded by splendid columns and arches gave onto the different garden areas, which led one into the other.

THE PALACES

The façades of the great fifteenth-century houses were embellished with stone carving. Although they feature classical elements brought from Italy, evidence of the humanistic culture of their owners, the stonework applied to the arches and door and window openings varied greatly, according to the different masonry schools appearing at that time throughout the region. The marked differences can be explained by the fact that from the time of the *Reconquista* through to the nineteenth century, Andalusia was divided into four great kingdoms: the Kingdom of Cordoba, the Holy Kingdom of Jaén (that included regions that belong today to the province of Albacete), the Kingdom of Granada (composed of the present provinces of Almería, Granada and Málaga) and the Kingdom of Seville (Seville, Cadiz and Huelva). The masons that worked in each kingdom – in most cases trained in Italy – imposed their individual interpretations of the Renaissance style on the houses of their region. These decisions were generally based on two premises: the preferences of the grandees who hired them and the influence other schools of thought may have had on their master masons. Masonry schools established themselves in a town to work on a major construction, such as a cathedral, that could last more than a century; the noblemen and civil and religious authorities from throughout the kingdom would go to the workshop to commission their building projects.

The limited communications between one region and another also contributed to the formation of mannerisms and the particular styles typical of each workshop. Thus, in the kingdom of Jaén (centred on its cities Jaén, Úbeda and Baeza), the influ-

CASA DE SALINAS A detail of the finely carved, interlaced designs on the arches of the courtyard.

ence of Castile prevailed because the manor houses were designed as an extension of the Castilian style. This is known as Gothic Plateresque, a late Gothic variation which became, in fact, the first Spanish Renaissance architecture.

Great architects soon became established in each region. In 1520, the Toledan Pedro Machuca arrived in Granada from Italy to paint the frescos of the Royal Chapel. Later, he worked on the Palace of Carlos V with Diego de Siloé, with whom he established a school. During the same period, an architect from Santander, Riaño, was working in Seville in a style which was rigid, but ornate. Hernán Ruiz, 'El Mozo', born in Cordoba and son of the master mason Hernán 'El Viejo', was a disciple of Riaño. And, in 1536, Andrés de Vandelvira, who was born in Alcaraz, arrived at Úbeda to continue the construction of the church of the Salvador, started by Siloé. Extremely productive all his life, Vandelvira worked mainly in the region of Jaén, and left impressive works of great architectural purity.

CASA DE MEDINA SIDONIA A corner of the courtyard, originally at the service entrance and designed for horses, seen from the loggia.

THE TOWNS SURROUNDING CASTILE

The kingdom of Jaén was linked to Castile by its proximity and by a similarity of character, but its buildings were very different from those of the rest of Andalusia. During the Renaissance, a custom known as *labrar la calle* was established in Jaén, whereby each citizen was responsible for the appearance of his section of the street and was to decorate his façade with pieces of hewn stone. Marble lintels and casings thus appeared on the house fronts, which were painted ochre to show up these details. Inside, however, the rooms were arranged in much the same way as they were in Sevillian houses. The differences in the façades was not fortuitous. Like Jaén, Úbeda and Baeza looked towards Castile and there the palaces rose over superb stone porticos. Seville, however, was influenced by the traditional Andalusian style, and its white-painted house fronts guarded courtyards and labyrinthine gardens.

Baeza and Úbeda are famous for their Gothic palaces, built when the first Castilians settled there, near to the lands they received in the distributions made after the Conquest. Then came the splendid palaces built during the Renaissance, financed by the economic expansion. Finally, halfway through the seventeenth century, the two cities were left suspended in time and building work declined.

The splendid palace of Jabalquinto, with its striking façade, was built in the fifteenth century. And it was in Baeza, and not in grand Úbeda, that even boasted a University, that Juan Alonso de Benevides, Lord of Jabalquinto and second cousin of Ferdinand the Catholic, ordered his palace to be built. Of its Gothic ground-plan, only the magnificent façade remains; it was commissioned by Don Alonso, designed by Enrique de Egea, and executed by the master mason Pedro López. The façade is composed of three parts: two Gothic sections and a Renaissance gallery, in imitation of the palaces of Úbeda. The first section is centred over the door, formed by an ogee arch resting on two columns, up which climb twisted human figures surrounded by fantastic motifs. The apex of the arch is the focal point which pulls together the design of the whole façade. The door is framed by two very subtle pinnacles, the whole forming a panel of the finest Gothic Plateresque. On either side, superb cylindrical buttresses rise to encircle the two Gothic sections in a false portal.

Little remains of its magnificent, rich interior. Only the polychrome coffered ceiling of the room with the largest window and the Renaissance courtyard are still intact. The repeated pattern of two children which appears on the arcade can also be seen decorating many of the capitals. From one end of the courtyard rises a baroque staircase with a semi-circular opening and some Romanesque columns taken from the church of San Juan. In 1720, the Counts of Benavente and the Marquis and Marquise of Jabalquinto donated the palace to be used as a seminary. The interior, emptied by then of works of art, underwent radical alterations to adapt it to its new educational function. In 1836, with Mendizábal's disenfranchisement, the palace became state owned.

The castle of Canena is equally elegant, rising impressively from the midst of a village of the same name on a hill by the road to Úbeda. It was built over the remains of a Roman fortress by the Arabs, who called it Hish Kenana, after the Arab lineage that settled there. Conquered by Ferdinand III ('the Saint') and quoted by the Marquis of Santillana in his ballads, the castle belonged at the time to the powerful military order of Calatrava. In 1538, it was bought by Francisco de los Cobos, who was born in Úbeda and became secretary and councillor to the Emperor Carlos V. Cobos ordered the castle to be remodelled in keeping with the style of the day, and summoned Andrés de Vandelvira to carry out the work. He designed the beautiful courtyard, with its square ground-plan and cubic towers at the corners, and the homage tower, which is today the stairwell. It also had great, three metre thick walls, a moat and drawbridge, but the latter has not survived.

The main entrance is a barrel arch flanked by Gothic Plateresque pilasters and capitals, above which a stone frieze with gargoyles is crowned by a semi-circlar moulding containing the coat-of-arms of the castle's founders. The arms courtyard, in which the great architect Vandelvira personally participated, has thirteen metre long sides, with Ionic columns and twenty-four barrel arches, surrounded by a Renaissance cloister decorated with high-relief medallions. This gallery opens onto rooms with magnificent wooden *artesonados*, and in one of them there is a lovely stone fireplace. Its present owners have made the castle habitable and the former moat has been converted into a small garden with a splendid view over the whole valley.

Úbeda, situated in the midst of the austere olive groves which cover the surrounding hills, is a beautiful, sleepy city, a jewel of Renaissance architecture, where time seems to have stopped. It is known as the Andalusian Salamanca. Úbeda reached its maximum splendour during the sixteenth century, under the reign of Carlos V, when the Castilian families started building palaces and churches there. They brought their own masons with them to erect houses similar in style to those of their home towns. The façades maintained the same Castilian Gothic Renaissance style, and nothing in them shows a hint of Moorish, or even Andalusian, influence.

A feature which marks these houses as different in style is that they are not designed for life to centre around the courtyards; in fact, most of the palace courtyards were walled up during the seventeenth century. Luckily, they were recovered later, although many of them were then fitted with stained-glass windows.

There are many palaces worth visiting in the city, but very few are still lived in. There are, however, two buildings, possibly not the most impressive, historically important or luxurious, that are still inhabited and are therefore worthy of special attention. The first is the Palacio de Molina del Postigo, also known as the Casa del Marqués de la Rambla, which has belonged to the same family since the sixteenth century. The other is the Palacio de Vela de Cobos, which in the nineteenth century became the property of the Sabater family, who carried out major alterations. The house has nevertheless retained its original magnificence, and history has not reduced it to a beautiful, proud, mysterious but, for all that, empty chest.

Opposite CASTILLO DE CANENA Built on top of the foundations of an old Arab fortress, the castle at Canena was restored in the sixteenth century by Andrés de Vandelvira. The sides of its impressive square courtyard are each thirteen metres long.

CASA DEL MARQUÉS DE SALVATIERRA, RONDA The main entrance doorway, ornate in style, contrasts with the austerity of the façade.

The palace of Vela de los Cobos is Vandelvira's second work in Úbeda and was built in 1560. It was commissioned by Don Francisco Vela de Cobos, chamberlain to Felipe II and member of a prominent family of the city. Only the façade of the building remains; neither the courtyard, with its double-columned arcade, nor the staircase, whose position and style changed over time, have survived. The main room, however, still has its Renaissance proportions and design. The façade has fewer decorative features than the palace of Vázquez de Molina, also designed by the brilliant Vandelvira, but they are richer. The lower section contains the main entrance, framed by a lintel and Corinthian columns. This floor is clearly separated from the one above by a cornice, which acts as base for all the ornamental elements of the second floor.

The second section, or main floor, is of Ionic order – Vandelvira had already used this inversion of architectural orders in the Vázquez de Molina palace – with four large monumental balconies, the most outstanding a corner one with a Tuscan column mullion and pediment shared by both streets, leaving an Ionic pilaster on either side. The second most striking balcony is the one which is a continuation of the entrance porch. Its shallow pediment rests on Ionic pilasters like the corner balcony. The pilasters follow the geometric order set by the porch columns and a young Atlantis rests on each one, with these unique supports rising from the triangular pediment. This balcony is flanked by a pair of matching balconies. The columns, either to reinforce the cornice or as simple adornment, rise from scroll-shaped brackets. It is interesting to note that the whole, fully Renaissance ornamentation in some ways heralds baroque forms. The third section rises high above a very marked cornice. This is a loggia composed of small barrel arches on pillars, with a central opening marking the door's axis. This gallery was the first to be built in Úbeda and its design became a typical feature of the town. Don Francisco Vela de Cobos was not able to enjoy his beautiful house for long, because he died in 1569, five years after the last recorded touches were in place.

In 1642, before the building was a hundred years old, its ownership changed hands. The palace was inherited by the Porcel family, who stayed at their Úbeda residence less and less, and the palace gradually fell into a derelict state. In 1873, the palace of Vela de los Cobos, by then in ruins, was purchased by the banker and politician Ignacio Sabater y Arauco. Don Ignacio started repairs and alterations and even bought new lands to extend the estate. The improvements included the garden portico, raised against the façade. When Don Ignacio died, the palace passed on to his daughter, Doña Maria. In 1939, Doña Patrocinio Sabatar – wife of Don Pedro Rivas, son of the politician Natalio Rivas – inherited the palace from her uncle; it now belongs to her son, Natalio Rivas Sabater, who carried out the latest general improvements in 1966.

The palace contains important documents about the different owners and a well cared-for library. Sabater also equipped the house with fine Spanish furniture of different periods, a good collection of oil paintings and a large number of extremely valuable objects.

Opposite PALACIO DE VELA DE LOS COBOS, ÚBEDA The staircase was restored in the last century to its original, Isabelline style. On the wall hangs a sixteenth-century Italian painting, *The Virgin of Bethlehem*. On the landing below, there are now a travelling counting-table and two folding travelling chairs.

PALACIO DE VELA DE LOS COBOS The street façade of the Palace, one of architect Andrés de Vandelvira's finest works. The entrance arch and the balconies of the first floor are particularly impressive. The corner balcony, with its mullion column and Ionic pilasters, is an unusual architectural feature.

PALACIO DE VELA DE LOS COBOS Valdés Leal (1622-90) painted the canvas of the *Inmaculada* which dominates the living room on the upper floor of the palace. Above the piano at the far end of the room is a painting of Santo Tomás de Villanueva by an artist of the Sevillian School, and on its left a head of San Francisco by the School of Ribera. The chairs are Louis XVI and the floral design carpet was made at the Real Fábrica – the Spanish royal factories.

PALACIO DE VELA DE LOS COBOS A view along the length of the dining room. The magnificent nineteenth-century chandelier is made of Bohemia glass and the room's mirrors and console-table are French. Above the table is an *Annunciation*, painted by an artist of the Sevillian School. The floor is paved with cut and polished marble and slate tiles.

Opposite PALACIO DE VELA DE LOS COBOS The palace library contains 9,000 of the 14,000 volumes kept in the house as a whole, including a significant collection of sixteenth-century incunabula and documents. An elaborate eighteenth-century bronze and ebony reliquary stands on the table on the right.

The Palacio de Molina del Postigo, or del Marqués de la Rambla, was built in the middle of the sixteenth century against the city walls, which themselves form part of the structure of several of its rooms. Although its present name refers to its latest owners, the Marquis and Marquise de la Rambla, this large, rambling house was originally commissioned by a member of the Molina family. The families are interconnected, as Captain Francisco de Molina y Valencia, lord of the small town of Ayorza, married Doña Mayor Vela de los Cobos, daughter of the owners of the palace of that name and ancestors of the first Marquis de la Rambla, Don José Sanvitores de la Portilla.

In November 1575, Captain Molina arranged for the local masons Juan de Madrid, Juan Hernández and his son Cristóbal to prepare the masonry stone required for the façade of his house near the Calancha gate. Around the same date, Juan and Christóbal Hernández were commissioned to make the porch window. Although Valdelvira had just died, his style still inspired the whole building, because Don Francisco Molina wanted his palace to be as similar as possible to his father-in-law's. And so it was. This system of commissioning the construction of the façade itself and its entrance arch separately was a new way of building and had decisive effects on other houses in the city.

The lower section of the façade has three windows above the wall foundations, finished with semi-circular mouldings and with the entrance porch situated at the end on the left. The porch has a lintel and is bordered by two free-standing Corinthian columns. The second section of the façade features two windows and a continuous, central balcony between two more openings.

The splendid courtyard has columns on the ground floor and a leaded, glass-covered loggia on the upper floor as protection against the intense cold. Only two sides of the courtyard are decorated with stonework – heraldic motifs and fantastic animals carved by the master mason, Esteban Jamete. The family coat-of-arms is carved on the upper part of the loggia and on the main façade. The position of the staircase is unusual, different from that of all other palaces in Úbeda, as it rises frontally from the courtyard and not in the more characteristic bend.

Some of the rooms on the ground floor still have their panels of Sevillian tiling, and a good collection of paintings from different periods decorates the walls, including portraits by Sotomayor and Moreno Carbonero. An unusual collection of eighteenth-century Spanish paper baskets is also on display. The living rooms, almost all in Isabelline style, lead off the gallery on the upper floor. The dining room is draped with red brocade, has a magnificent coffered ceiling and contains a collection of West Indies Company china. King Alfonso XIII stayed at the palace when visiting the region. During the Civil War, it suffered severe damage, which was recently restored by the architect Pedro Ponce de León, who updated the electrical and sanitary systems and improved the roofs and carpentry. Some of the palace's rooms are now open to the public.

In the city of Úbeda itself, the eighteenth-century decadence which condemned it to silence and oblivion is evident. There were no more Cobos, no more potentate Molinas. The Court was firmly established in Madrid and the noble families of Úbeda, Granada and Seville hurried there to build themselves new mansions on the shores of the river Manzanares. Some Andalusian towns were more affected than others by the departure of their lords, but Úbeda suffered badly from the exodus.

CORDOBA

By the tenth century, Cordoba was seen to have achieved earthly perfection as capital of the Caliphate under the Umayyad dynasty. According to the chroniclers, it had at the time about one million inhabitants, two hundred thousand houses, six hundred mosques and nine hundred baths, all in a walled city surrounded by the river Guadalquivir. Here the most beautiful and the richest mosques that ever existed were built with stones and columns brought up the river in barges from the Roman and Visigoth palaces dismantled in Seville. (Such was this Moorish opulence that seven kilometres away a dream summer city, Medina Azahara, was built as a present for a favourite of the Caliph, with palaces, gardens, fountains and flowers.)

A civilization flourished under the aegis of this Caliphate that reached heights that would never again be equalled. Physicians, poets, philosophers, astronomers and scholars all developed their learning here. Aristoteles was translated, religions were respected and all lived in harmony under just rulers who forbade serfdom and distributed the taxes fairly. Ever since the rule of Abd ar-Rahman, Cordoba had had paved streets, public lighting, channelled water systems and many buildings of which nothing has survived. Its largest mansions were hardly visible, reluctant to exhibit themselves; no palaces were built, only great houses in a city that had been the centre of an Empire.

The enormous weight of this history is perhaps the price Cordoba has since had to pay; having once received such an excess of architectural gifts, the city can never forget its past glory. The Cordoban Renaissance palaces that have survived do not have such important architectural features as those of Úbeda or Seville. Their façades are not as interesting as the magnificent stone fronts of Úbeda and usually go unnoticed behind limewashed walls, sometimes interrupted by railings that allow a glimpse of splendid courtyards and gardens beyond. The Casa de los Herruzo, for example, has seven courtyards and the famous Palacio de Viana has twelve.

However, the entrance arches of the palaces are as varied in character as their owners. Some are formed by marble adornments like those of the palaces of Úbeda, and on others, the carved stone porch is embedded in a limewashed masonry wall. Others combine Renaissance and Mudéjar elements, and some show a mixture of Italianized ornamentation on fully Gothic structures.

Inside, they all maintain the popular Andalusian design centred around one or more courtyard. But the Cordoban courtyards are different from those found in Seville or Úbeda. Their flat arches with lintels remind one more of the porticos of La Mancha. Such a design is found in the courtyards of both popular houses and great mansions, although the latter sometimes feature classical, landscaped and porticoed courtyards instead.

The Cordoban palaces, even the grandest, like the house of the Marquises of Viana, rarely contained the Sevillian *apeadero*, or carriage entrance. Neither have any large porticoed loggias survived, except in ruins, and those documented used uncarved capitals or ones taken wholesale from some Muslim building. Perhaps the Cordoban aristocracy felt no need to display their wealth and power as Úbeda's did, or was in fact less powerful than the Enríquez of Seville.

As a result, the palaces built in Cordoba were freer, more modest and more personal in style. They might have Gothic façades, like that of the Bailío mansion, or simple, almost exquisite fronts, such as that of the Mudéjar-type house of the Aguayos. In a loose comparison, a Cordoban palace has more in common with its Sevillian counterpart than it does with its equivalent in Úbeda. This similarity is in its harmonious combination of Moorish and Castilian styles, whereas the Úbeda façades were robust panels of freestone built in a severely defined style – either totally Plateresque or fully Renaissance – but with no concessions made to Moorish 'impurities'. The Cordobans freely combined hewn stone with masonry walls and built Mudéjar mullioned windows next to Roman telamones without any fuss about the mix of styles.

Cordoban courtyards, from the grandest mansions to the humblest house, were real gems of landscaped gardens in the Arab tradition. They retained the traditional art of water, making it follow an intricate path from the spout, jumping from courtyard to courtyard, down steps, filling pools and irrigating orchards and vegetable gardens. These courtyards were designed for pleasure, with fountains and oranges, lemons or grapefruits growing within hand's reach. The ground was either stone-paved or *enchinado*, that is, covered with two colours of river pebbles forming carpet-like designs, often combined with brick paths in herringbone patterns and flanked by canals or flowerbeds. The interiors also pay homage to the past, which nobody in this city can, or wishes, to cast aside.

The oldest part of the Casa de los Marqueses de Viana dates back to the fourteenth century, although the beautiful corner entrance arch was built in the sixteenth century. It was commissioned by the Marqueses of Villaseca and kept in the family until 1980. Together with the mansions belonging to Jerónimo Páez, the Marquis de la Fuensanta and the Villalones, it is one of the most important houses of the city.

Its exterior gives no hint of what will be found inside, except that the Renaissance façade, in the middle of the popular district of Santa Marina de Agua Santa, is an indication that this is no ordinary house. It is composed of a central section onto which several adjacent houses have been added in the course of time,

Opposite PALACIO DE VIANA, CORDOBA
The gate courtyard (*patio de la cancela*), porticoed and with large stone pillars, opens onto the street.

PALACIO DE VIANA The reception courtyard (*patio del recibo*) is the first of this palace's twelve

courtyards. It boasts classical columns and a magnificent black and white pebble-mosaic floor.

PALACIO DE VIANA Rich planting around the fountain in the *patio de los Naranjos*

includes hundred-year-old orange trees and brilliant flowering wysteria and heliotropes.

PALACIO DE VIANA An eighteenth-century Gobelin
tapestry, illustrating 'The transport of sugar cane'.

PALACIO DE VIANA Another eighteenth-century
Gobelin tapestry, depicting 'The fight of the animals'.

PALACIO DE VIANA One of the palace's rooms is hung with a magnificent tapestry by Francisco Goya y Lucientes, *Zancos* (stilts). On the right, part of an eighteenth-century Teniers tapestry from the Real Fábrica de Santa Bárbara is visible. The gold and white upholstered chairs are Carlos IV.

PALACIO DE VIANA A view of the lavish 'Neo-classical' room. Ornate Sèvres china, including a clock and candelabra, are exhibited on the mantelpiece.

PALACIO DE VIANA A sparsely-furnished guest room, also known as the Admiral's Room. Above the Empire marquetry head-board is a Flemish painting board of Calvary by Frans Francken II. On the Renaissance chest-of-drawers stands a faded, polychrome figure of Santa Bárbara.

Opposite PALACIO DE VIANA The 'Neo-classical' room is decorated with stucco mouldings on the cornice and ceiling. Charming allegorical monotone paintings illustrating the Senses are inset on the walls. *Arte Povera* chairs and a pedestal table are collected in an intimate corner. The vivid upholstery is of blue damask.

gradually forming the palace's famous twelve courtyards. Access is through the corner entrance, which is topped by a balcony flanked by two warriors and with the Argote and Figueroa coats-of-arms, and, higher up, the Saavedra crest with the family motto, *Padecer por Vivir* (Suffer to Live). The house has a typical Cordoban structure, designed like all Andalusian houses for the hot climate, with the upper floor used in winter and the lower one during summer.

Its rooms and loggias house a complete and magnificent collection of works of art, from ninth-century Visigoth consoles, Gothic chests and collections of sixteenth- and seventeenth-century weapons to paintings by Joaquin Sorolla. The magnificent Gobelin tapestries are of particular interest, as they represent the five continents, and there is an extraordinary Goya tapestry, brought here from the family's Madrid residence (which now houses the Ministry of Foreign Affairs). The house also has collections of Meissen, Compañía de Indias and Saxony china-ware and embossed leather articles, pottery and carpets. The variety of pavings is amazing, ranging from Roman mosaics and Italian marbles in the drawing rooms to the simplest of clay tiles in less important areas of the house. The palace remained in the family of the Marquis of Viana until the 1980s, when it was bought by a financial society that has opened it to the public.

Opposite PALACIO DEL MARQUÉS DEL CARPIO, CORDOBA
This key-hole shaped Arab arch is the oldest in the
house and leads into the main courtyard.

PALACIO DEL MARQUÉS DEL CARPIO The Patio de la Huerta (orchard), one of
the seven courtyards of this palace. The ancient pool was originally built as
a reservoir. The palace itself rises up behind orange and palm trees.

Opposite PALACIO DEL MARQUÉS DEL CARPIO
The centre of the main courtyard, with its
Arab fountain. Esparto mats hang between the
columns as protection against the summer heat.

PALACIO DEL MARQUÉS DEL CARPIO A classical
deity looks out across the courtyard from a
pedestal composed of fragments of Roman
columns. A beautiful, *fleur-de-lis*, pebble mosaic
radiates out around him.

PALACIO DEL MARQUÉS DEL CARPIO A section of
the stone and brickwork façade of the
fifteenth-century tower.

PALACIO DEL MARQUÉS DEL CARPIO *The library is dominated by a painting of the* Immaculate Conception *by Palomino (1655–1726). Its showcases exhibit a collection of Roman coins, glass perfume bottles, enamelled objects and incunabula.*

The fifteenth-century house of the Marqués del Carpio, unnoticed in the calle de las Cabezas, is another grand pa[...] was purchased in 1924 by Don Antonio Herruzo Martos and D[...] who recently carried out restoration and improvement works a[...] which are an example of neo-Mudéjar architecture. The garde[...] landscaped in the best Cordoban tradition.

The fifteenth-century tower-house rises proudly from [...] all the simplicity and firmness of masonry stone. It has a[...] front and the windows are shaded by *esparto* rugs against the[...]

A Moorish horseshoe arch connects the courtyard, a[...] one of the oldest parts of the house, which is decorated[...] fered ceiling, and which opens onto the *venison loggia*, s[...] columns surmounted by Caliphal capitals. The beauty of the [...]

[Overlaid newspaper clipping:]

e *time*

[...]ntecito Water Board, arguing [...]te water was too expensive, los[...] good old boys. "I wanted to rec[...] [...]ntecito's entitlement because I [...]nk we could afford it." Now, she [...]e district budget has swelled from [...]illion to $10 million, half of it to p[...] [...]r state water.

In 1991, Kreiger and Sjovold were [...]oices of reason shouted down or [...]gnored by the panicked and the pr[...] [...]teers. People, she says, "didn't belie[...] [...]us."

Now many wish they'd listened instead of believing in a mirage.

with orange and grapefruit trees and privet hedges, takes one by surprise. This pebble-paved courtyard in turn leads to others of different sizes, one with a well and a hunting scene set in the paving, another with a swimming pool, the next an orchard garden and so on, to a total of seven courtyards, all with pools, fountains and water spouts.

Remains of Roman pottery and of Arab *ajimeces* (mullioned windows) found in the house have been framed and set in the walls. The most noteworthy features of the interior are the *artesonados* of the dining hall, office, the library and the French Room, with their clay-tiled floors and ceramic-tiled friezes.

SEVILLE

Founded by Hercules and conquered by Caesar, Seville was the capital of Andalusia at the time of the Visigoths, capital of its own kingdom under the Arabs, capital of Castile under Ferdinand and the richest city in Europe when it was the customs post of trade with the West Indies. This is the city of Don Juan and of Carmen, and here, there is no doubt, the *duende* prevails.

In the architecture of great houses, Seville has followed its own standards and generated a style as original as it was prolific and which lasted and evolved for three centuries, from the fifteenth to the eighteenth. This does not mean that the Sevillian aristocracy and their architects were not familiar with the palaces of Baeza, Úbeda and Jaén, or with their excellent masons; it simply means that they had created a particular type of residence that they found more pleasing. They admired the finesse and the elegance of the Jaén stonework, and it is worth noting that Hernán Ruiz II, who was considered possible successor of Andrés de Vandelvira, came to work in Seville.

Hernán Ruiz was a highly promising young master mason who was hired by the builders' guild of the cathedral of Seville. His best works were done here between 1556 and 1569, the year of his death. During this brief time, he published a treaty on architecture, built the famous Giraldillo and the superb Chapter House of the cathedral and – perhaps his crowning work – designed the Hospital de la Sangre. He also took part in the construction of the City Hall. He must have been as tireless as he was ambitious, because during the last seven years of his life, until he died of fevers at the age of thirty-seven, he had occupied all the prominent positions of his profession and took charge of the rest of the architects in Seville at the time. Another master mason from Jaén who settled in the kingdom of Seville was Alfonso de Valdelvira, son of the brilliant Andrés Valdelvira.

While the palace of Jaén was designed under Castilian influence, that of Seville was affected by the admiration the Seville aristocracy felt for King Pedro's Reales Alcázares, the Moorish palace of Ronda (it has not survived and it is thought that the palace of Salvatierra is built on its site) and for the Red Palace of the Alhambra. The Seville palaces emulate the royal Moorish constructions and dress their interiors in Mudéjar style.

PALACIO DEL MARQUÉS DEL CARPIO One of two Roman columns with Corinthian capitals that flanked the entrance to the original *apeadero*.

This reverence for Moorish architecture was caused by a historical coincidence. The first three Sevillian palaces were commissioned at the same time as Granada was conquered. To start with, Ferdinand and Isabel had to stay in the Alcázares of Seville while preparing the campaign. Then, when Ronda was conquered, they established their grand headquarters in its palace – that the King very much admired – until moving to Santa Fe for the siege of Granada. And, finally, the sovereigns and the Court settled in the captivating Alhambra of the conquered city. The first to be impressed by the Mudéjar architecture were the King and Queen, so the Sevillian nobility hired the best *alarifes* in Granada and the south of Andalusia to adapt their houses to the royal tastes. A semantic point is worth mentioning here: the Andalusian noblemen referred to their mansions as *casas* to establish a respectful distinction from *palacios*, which would be applied exclusively to the royal residences.

Thus the Sevillian mansions were originally built as copies of the Moorish palaces, as can be seen in the oldest rooms of the Casa de Pilatos and of the Casa de las Dueñas: simple, limewashed walls on the outside, with sparse stone carving, and lavish interiors surrounded by a network of connecting gardens and courtyards. This may have been the initial proposal, but the works took such a long time that new concepts in building and decoration influenced by the Italian Renaissance were also introduced in the construction.

One of the three first stately houses to be erected in the city, and of which practically nothing remains, was commissioned by a Genoese, Francisco de Pinelli, banker of the Catholic Sovereigns and future Factor of the *Aduana de América*. Pinelli (or Pinelo), expert in Renaissance art, directly introduced splendid Italian ornamentation to his house. Another monument that impressed the city's inhabitants was the fantastic tomb of the archbishop Don Diego Hurtado de Mendoza in the cathedral, built in 1509 by the Italian artist Domenico Fancello. The Sevillian aristocracy immediately wanted their palaces to include such marvellous new stonework. The resident Genoese artists received the commissions, and thus the Italian Renaissance arrived in Seville without any adaptations of its decorative styles.

These two architectural elements – the general Moorish ground-plan and the incorporation of Italian ornamentation – were constant and accentuated the differences in style between the manor houses of Seville and those of Jaén. The two styles each became increasingly defined and developed at a tangent to each other.

Seville became the bright architectural jewel of Europe and its nobility, with limitless amounts of money at its disposal, one of the most ostentatious and lavish. Its palaces became exoticized models of the traditional Andalusian house. On a more modest scale, the less grand houses built in the city during its great seventeenth-century urban development, when a large part of the city walls was pulled down, were similarly designed; and so were the baroque mansions raised on the shores of the Guadalquivir. They may have been smaller, but they were certainly no less pretentious or exuberantly ornamented.

PALACIO DE LAS DUEÑAS Vivid magenta geraniums flower in a glazed pot in the gardens. The decoration typically incorporates the name of the house and the family coat-of-arms.

PALACIO DE LAS DUEÑAS Bougainvillaea in full flower against the façade.

Instead of leaving the town to be nearer the Court, the Sevillian nobility settled near their dominions within the kingdom to keep an eye on their crops and to enjoy their delightful city. Seville was quite different in spirit to needy and austere seventeenth-century Madrid, with its El Escorial Court, and was still famous for its gaiety, its celebrations and for the possibilities it offered of making a fortune. The increasing number of noble families wishing to settle here required the construction of new houses until well into the eighteenth century, as long as goods in boundless quantities kept coming from America. The noblemen lived on their huge, untaxed incomes until the dominion of the oceans transferred firmly in favour of England.

The architecture of Seville's Renaissance palaces was based on specific ground-plans and on a series of architectural features for which it would become famous. The first characteristic elements of the buildings were the carriage entrances, known as *picaderos* or *apeaderos*, clear yards of any shape but usually occupying the whole façade, used for preparing the family's carriages and horses. An *apeadero* was protected from the outside by a high wall, with the entrance arch opening onto the street. The coach shed, stables and saddle rooms were built against the wall in independent annexes. The *apeadero* had direct access to the house,

PALACIO DE LAS DUEÑAS This passage room, which runs from the entrance to the main courtyard, is decorated with paintings, posters and heads celebrating bulls and bullfighting. The blue and white ceramic tiles to dado height were made in Seville.

PALACIO DE LAS DUEÑAS The Sevillian tiles, ceramic inset with metallic chips, that pave and skirt the antechapel are amongst the oldest in the house, dating from the sixteenth century. The polychrome painted wooden ceiling is well preserved, and there are remains of mural paintings on the walls. There is striking plasterwork on the picture frames and wall friezes.

PALACIO DE LAS DUEÑAS Magnificent stonework friezes and cornices and sixteenth-century tiles are seen here in the [...] chapel

Opposite PALACIO DE LAS DUEÑAS [...] vaulted chapel is decorated with [...] century tiles on both the walls a[...] The altarpiece by Neri de Bicci [...] dedicated to Saint Catherine of [...]

PALACIO DE LAS DUEÑAS The opulent 'Square Room' is dominated by an embroidered hanging with the Alvarez de Toledo coat-of-arms. The flat wooden ceiling is surrounded by a double cornice frieze, one part wooden and the other carved stone. The floor is made of earthenware tiles inset with blue ceramic wedges.

either through a front door in the main building or via one or two side doors leading to the servants' quarters. In some cases, a reception room, *antesala*, on the first floor had a large window, *mirador*, looking over the *apeadero*.

The main courtyard, *gran patio*, is the second element typical of a Sevillian Renaissance palace. Based on Moorish tradition and on King Pedro's Royal Alcázares, it could be approached either along an 'L'-shaped passage or through a small guard room that two centuries later would become the *casapuerta*, or entrance hall. During the Renaissance, the *apeadero* and this first lobby were usually unadorned, but iron grilles, lanterns and glazed tiles later decorated the baroque *casapuerta*. The main courtyard was the most important room of the house, combining elegant Italian architecture with Mudéjar ornamentation. It was here that the master of the house received his guests, clients and protégés, where receptions were held in the summer and where all the important events of the palace took place. It usually contained a Moorish fountain and was surrounded by the traditional arrangement of double living-quarters. It led off into other independent buildings, such as the palace chapel or oratory (often built, oddly enough, on the site of former Roman *lares*), a summer dining hall and perhaps an administrative office.

The purpose of this courtyard was to glorify the owner of the house, so it was designed with appropriate magnificence. The decoration was, inevitably,

PALACIO DE LAS DUEÑAS A view along the beaten earth path of an arcade in one of the lush gardens of the palace. Orange and lemon trees and cypress bushes lead to a ceramic-tiled fountain.

Moorish, as this was the style of the courtyard de Arrayanes at the Alhambra. Here, the cunning arrangement of the interconnecting courtyards obliged ambassadors to arrive at the Throne Room in a roundabout way. The splendid decorations of Pedro I's Patio de las Doncellas in the Royal Alcázares was another Moorish model, with its royal study adjoining the courtyard, which had been built by the best craftsmen of Granada with the intention of surprising and amazing the Castilian aristocracy.

The courtyard was embellished with a double-porticoed gallery leading onto all the main areas of the house, according to Renaissance standards. Its double cloister was the palace's vital artery. In the architecture of these loggias, Seville blended both styles, Italian Renaissance and Moorish Andalusian, with ease. The combination reached great architectural heights, creating a unique style which was known as Sevillian and which eventually affected all the elements of the building, including the tiled dados and panels, in which spans of typically Moorish, geometrical laceries were spliced with grotesques and with vegetable motifs of Tuscan origin.

The rest of the courtyards, if any, formed separate modules of the mansion, leading off from disparate alcoves and living-quarters. These were often lovelier, more secluded and poetical than the grand patio, because their mission was not to impress but simply to provide pleasure and delight.

Another component characteristic of the Renaissance palace of Seville was the garden, which led off from the main courtyard. It was designed to interconnect the remaining courtyards and to make the life of the noble household more agreeable. Later on, towards the middle of the sixteenth century, it usually incorporated statues, fountains and a landscaping loaded with classical symbolism. But the gardens of the Sevillian mansions could never resemble the vast and stately Palatine gardens of Italy, which were laid out in esoteric mazes, leading the walker along intricate paths. The gardens of the Sevillian manor house were of reduced proportions, with a hint of Arabic mysticism, but also, thanks to their position at the back of the main floor of the house, they had a far more down-to-earth atmosphere.

As well as providing a comfortable ascent to the first floor – and the palace, of course, had other, secondary stairs leading to different areas of the building – the main staircase also served as a second entrance hall, usually 'L'-shaped and with fully Moorish decoration. Here, the panels of ceramic tiling, the Mozarabic coffers (*casetones*) and the lofty, beamed ceilings (*alfarjes*) were designed to dazzle visitors to the palace.

Three houses built in Seville at the end of the fifteenth century are particularly worthy of mention: the Palacio de Pinelo, Casa de Pilatos and Palacio de las Dueñas. While Pinelo was building his palace, Pilatos and Dueñas were also under construction and their architects eager to introduce Renaissance elements ordered from Genoa, such as the entrance arch of Pilatos, or its marble columns and paving slabs.

Little has survived of Pinelo's mansion, but it deserves a special place in the architecture of the great houses of Seville. The palace of Pinelo is not the earliest to be commissioned, but it was the first to be completed. The ground-plan of the palace of las Dueñas is undoubtedly earlier and whole sections of the Casa de Pilatos are, if not older, at least contemporaneous. But, because of its completion date, and as a result of the influence it had on the two other buildings, Pinelo's must be considered the first Sevillian Renaissance manor house. It was certainly the first to introduce genuinely Italian Renaissance features to its decoration. Such audacity naturally caused a certain commotion, but in view of the owner's rank and royal standing, indignation turned to flattery and, finally, to imitation. Pinelo became Ferdinand and Isabel's grand banker and as such acted as the royal purse for the military campaigns of Granada, Naples and the Canary Isles. His support of Columbus' first and second voyages earned him the title of Factor of the newly founded *Casa de Contratacion* (a planning centre for the colonisation of the Indies) in 1503.

The banker ordered his house to be built (in what is now the *calle Abades*) according to Italian Renaissance standards, and records describe how the house was full of marble surfaces, unusual in that marble was generally used for more specific structural and decorative devices, such as columns, mullions and busts. Unfortunately, very little has survived of the original house, apart from the courtyard loggia, which displays a lovely combination of different white marbles, and the Mozarabic plasterwork. The openings of the loggia arches are crowned with Moorish decorations which are repeated in Las Dueñas and Pilatos. Their style is obviously not Renaissance, but is itself in imitation of the arcades of the Alcázares. However, the spandrels of the arches are embellished here for the first time with stone medallions containing carved male figures from antiquity, a motif popular in Italy at the time and one which Pinelo introduced to Seville. This type of medallion must have been well received, because it was immediately used in the Casa de las Torres of Úbeda, although with far rougher stonework.

By combining both styles, Pinelo had, then, invented the Sevillian style. Given the Genoese banker's influence, it is not far-fetched to think that if he had rejected Moorish ornamentation and proclaimed it too elaborate and in bad taste, contrary to the rectilinear and vigorous Renaissance styles of Italy, part of the Sevillian nobility would have followed his example and spurned the Moorish style.

The Palacio de las Dueñas, residence of the Alba, is named after the nearby monastery of Santa Maria de las Dueñas and has been described as less ostentatious than Pilatos, but surpassing it in harmony, delicacy and distinction.

The palace belonged to the Pineda family, Lords of Casa Bermeja, who sold it urgently in 1483 to Doña Catalina de Ribera, wife of Don Pedro Enríquez, governor of Andalusia, who also owned the Casa de Pilatos. The sale was pressing because Don Juan de Pineda had been captured by the Moors after the failed conquest of the Ajarquía of Malaga. To raise money for the heavy ransom demanded by the Muslims for the life of the Lord of Casa Bermeja, the family put the property up for sale.

The Palacio de las Dueñas was inherited by the House of Alba. In the sixteenth and seventeenth centuries, the estate was involved in the extravagant life of Seville, but, like all the great Andalusian houses, it suffered a slow but constant decline from the eighteenth century onwards. By the nineteenth century, the Albas established their residence in the Palacio de Liria in Madrid and their visits to the valley of the Guadalquivir became increasingly less frequent. This tendency applied to all the grandees of their time: during the 'Century of Enlightment', Court obligations took them no further than the Río Frío to the north and Aranjuez to the south, because the monarchs, the Court and the State had become extremely centralist and great lovers of the Guadarrama; also, the fierce political changes of the restless nineteenth century made it advisable not to move around much and to be on the alert.

Towards the end of the turbulent century, however, one Empress did spend long periods in the palace: Doña Eugenia María de Montijo y de Guzmán, Napoleon III's wife. The palace became steeped in the legend of this dethroned Empress, who the Andalusians always regarded with respect and devotion, as she came from Granada and because she was wrapped in a suitable shroud of melancholy because of her abduction, her widowhood and the loss of her son.

Other famous names associated with the palace are Manuel and Antonio Machado, the latter possibly Spain's most popular twentieth-century poet, in the best sense of the word. Don Antonio wrote: 'I was born in Seville one July night in 1875, in the famous Palacio de las Dueñas, situated in the street of the same name'; a year before, his brother Manuel was also born there. Don Antonio Machado Álvarez, great folklorist and father of the two poets, had rented rooms in the Alba property in a separate annexe off the main courtyard. Even a garden was included in the contract, which Don Antonio described in a poem:

> Esta luz de Sevilla...Es el palacio
> donde nací, con su rumor de fuente.
> Mi padre, en su despacho -la alta frente,
> la breve mosca, y el bigote lacio-.
> Mi padre aún joven. Lee, escribe, hojea
> sus libros y medita. Se levanta:
> va hacia la puerta del jardín. Pasea.
> A veces solo, a veces canta.

His poem describes his father working in his office in the palace, reading, writing and lost in thought. The sound of the fountain outside is clearly heard, and his father gets up and goes through the door to walk in the garden. Sometimes, the poet can hear his father, still a young man sporting a goatee beard and straight moustache, singing to himself in the garden.

CASA DE SALINAS The ceramic-tiled wall panels and brick floor of the main courtyard date from the sixteenth century. The central fountain is Moorish.

These leasing arrangements show how uninterested the Albas were in the palace at that time. However, the next Duke, Don Jacobo Fitz-James Stuart, remedied the situation by carrying out extensive sanitary improvements to the palace, which is now in perfect condition – so much so that it is the Duchess of Alba's favourite residence and she spends possibly more time here than at her house in Madrid.

The severe architecture of the main entrance is in keeping with the Sevillian style. It is formed by an arch with the Alba coat-of-arms painted on tiles, instead of the usual hewn-stone proclamation. It dates, surprisingly, from the end of the sixteenth century or the beginning of the seventeenth century, when the palace had already been in the family for forty or fifty years.

Behind the entrance arch and adjacent to the *picadero* is the first garden, planted with orange and palm trees. At the other side of this garden is a curved passage leading to the main courtyard, around which the main rooms of the house are arranged, which in turn are totally surrounded by more gardens, to form a complex network. The main courtyard is porticoed on all four sides, with beautiful arcades on both floors, decorated with Renaissance plasterwork and open-work balustrades. Around these are two large, rectangular rooms, the summer dining hall and the chapel, which is clearly Plateresque, with its plaster moulding in imitation of carved granite and its stucco access arch. Inside the chapel, the sagged vault ribs cross over the quadrangular room and break off to lean on four brackets held up by Gothic angels. This is possibly one of the oldest rooms of the house.

The main rooms are on the upper floor. They contain countless treasures, some bequeathed by the Empress Eugenia. The extensive collection of paintings covers several periods, including two splendid portraits of Napoleon III and Eugenia de Montijo by Franz Xavier Wintherhalter, works by Federico Madrazo and good, Spanish baroque paintings. There is also a collection of seventeenth- and eighteenth-century jewellery and some domestic objects of exquisite craftmanship.

The transitional areas, like stairs and antechambers, are decorated with Sevillian tile panels with clearly Moorish patterns. But the most striking decorations are the coffered and cross-beamed ceilings of the great living rooms and stairs, which are perhaps unrivalled. The intricate Andalusian carpentry, framed by Mozarabic fascias in a combination of wood and plaster, are unique, and in an excellent state of conservation

The Casa de Pilatos – also called Palacio de San Andrés or Palacio del Marqués de Tarifa – is the third important house of this period in Seville. Its construction was started at the end of the fifteenth century by Don Pedro Enríquez, Governor of Andalusia, and his wife Catalina de Ribera. Their son, Fadrique Enríquez de Ribera, then continued the building work, which was completed sixty years later by Don Per Afán Enríquez de Ribera, Duke of Alcalá, Ambassador to the Pope and nephew of Don Fadrique.

CASA DE MORENO DE LA COVA, SEVILLE
A wall-mounted collection of small china birds of different origin is displayed in an anteroom to a bedroom. On the right is a splendid Sevillian baroque image of the young Christ, *El Niño Jesús del Remedio.*

The mansion covers an area of about 10,000 square metres. During its construction, adjoining properties were added, preventing the building from being a homogenous project in the modern sense of the term. Later, other inheritors continued modifying the building and shaping the present multi-form appearance of the estate. But however many different styles and periods the house reflects, the overall result is of prodigious charm and is full of surprises.

The plans drawn up for Don Pedro Enríquez and Doña Catalina de Ribera were clearly inspired by Mudéjar palaces and partly copied the plans of the Alhambra and, in particular, the Reales Alcázares. However, their son, Don Fadrique, later radically altered the decorative design by introducing Italian Renaissance ornamentation without reserve.

The construction is unique and monumental. In some ways, the Palacio de San Andrés is the inspirational source of the Andalusian baroque style. The origin of the name Pilatos dates back to a visit Don Fadrique made to the Holy Land. On his return, the first Marquis of Tarifa wrote his *Viaje a Jerusalén*, in which he describes the Roman *praetorium* in great detail. He stresses the fact that the distance from the door of the palace of San Andrés to the Calvary known as the Cruz del Campo – built in a Mudéjar Gothic by Diego Merlo in 1482 – was the

CASA DE MORENO DE LA COVA A bedroom with Carlos IV mahogany beds topped by a pink silk canopy.

CASA DE MORENO DE LA COVA A sixteenth-century Flemish folding campaign oratory altarpiece in the lower loggia.

Opposite CASA DE MORENO DE LA COVA A detail of the central panel of the altarpiece.

same as the distance separating Pontius Pilate's assumed *praetorium* from Golgotha. Impressed by such a coincidence, he ordered a Via Crucis to be constructed, leading from the door of the mansion to the said small temple, giving rise to the house's popular name of Casa de Pilatos.

In 1533, the entrance arch, the fountains and the columns for the main courtyard arrived from Genoa on a ship that sailed up the Guadalquivir: the Italian Renaissance entered the Casa de Pilatos the grand way. On the same ship were the master masons who had carved the stones: Antonio María de Aprile de Carona, his brother Juan Antonio Aprile and Pace Gazziani. Don Fadrique had commissioned this stonework when passing through Genoa on his journey to the Holy Land. The entrance arch was immediately erected and resembled an elegant triumphal arch. It is formed by two simple pilasters with Corinthian capitals, surmounted by two medallions with heads of emperors to guard the entrance. The Castilian custom was usually to place sculptures of monsters as guardians of the family lineage, and his leap to the use of Roman emperors instead points to Don Fadrique's

preferences and aspirations and to his intention of converting the Casa de
Pilatos into a classical Temple of Fame.

The main courtyard is fully Renaissance, in spite of its exhuberant
Mudéjar decoration. It forms an almost perfect square, with sides measuring twenty-
five metres, with a double-porticoed loggia. Surprisingly, only six of the thirty
possible capitals are lightly carved. The whole arcade rests on Carrara marble
columns cut by the Aprile brothers. The arches are decorated with Mudéjar stucco
and pieces of Arabic lettering, showing a full acceptance of Moorish style and culture. The fountain, crowned by a two-faced bust of Janus, also a work of the Genoese
masons, marks the exact centre of the courtyard.

The most striking element of the courtyard's loggias is their tiled panels, carried out by the Polido brothers between 1535 and 1538 under a contract signed
with the Marquis of Tarifa. This agreement applied to all the tiles of the house,

CASA DE MORENO DE LA COVA A charming Neapolitan Nativity scene in the 'Piano Room'.

CASA DE MORENO DE LA COVA The 'Piano Room' is dominated by a chandelier from La Granja. The pictures either side of the fireplace represent the *Seises* – choir boys of Seville cathedral dressed for the Corpus celebration – and the Virgin Mary.

CASA DE MORENO DE LA COVA One of the house's courtyards, with its Genoese columns, second-century Roman sculptures and seventeenth-century tiles.

which covered a total surface area of 1,200 square metres. The Polido brothers employed two techniques in the fabrication of the panels: the ancient one of using dry rope and the more modern basin system. The tiles show three main motifs: the well-known Mudéjar stars, bows, chains and other threaded patterns; Isabelline motifs inspired by the tapestries of the period; and a handful of fully Renaissance motifs, such as scrolls, acanthus and grotesques.

Other buildings in Seville dating from the same period include the Casa de Salinas and the Casa de Moreno de la Cova, both inspired by the Casa de Pilatos and by Dueñas. Together, they became the established model for new buildings of the period.

The Casa de Salinas is close to the district of Santa Cruz, very near the Giralda. It dates back to the sixteenth century and was built by Jaén Roelas, although it has

undergone frequent alterations since. However, certain of its features still show the influence of the style introduced at Dueñas and Pilatos, such as the 'L'-shaped entrance passage, the courtyards and the iron gratings. Inside, it still boasts a beautiful balustrade of Carrara marble, sculpted with lions and made in one piece. The courtyard contains panels of sixteenth-century Sevillian tiles and the original main staircase. The first-floor loggia has lovely mahogany-framed glass windows. The second courtyard – a former kitchen garden – contains a famous second-century mosaic from Italica, a stone Roman head that was part of the collection of the Marquis of Aracena and a Madonna from the Convento de los Remedios.

In 1880, the house was bought by Don Eduardo Ibarra and was restored by Gestoso, who followed the prevailing fashion of the time by equipping the old Renaissance house with modern features. In 1930, it was purchased by the Salinas family, to whom it owes it current name and recent restorations.

The façade of the house of Moreno de la Cova in the calle Guzmán el Bueno stands out from the others in the narrow street because of its splendid sixteenth-century marble entrance arch. The house has had several owners since its construction. It was the British Consulate at the beginning of this century and in the thirties was bought by its present owners, an old stock-breeding family.

The marble entrance is flanked by Ionic columns on pedestals, with vegetable motifs decorating the shafts and brackets holding up a balcony over the lintel. Behind the entrance arch, a half-covered yard with stables leads through an iron gate to the courtyard, which is surrounded by white Italian marble columns and has a marble well in its centre and two second-century Roman statues in the corners. The courtyard is porticoed on all four sides; on the ground floor, semicircular arches are decorated with plasterwork and on the upper floor, the balconies are separated by pilasters. The lower gallery opens onto several large rooms, including a library housing a large number of books about bull-fighting and a chapel. One of the rooms off the lower arcade opens onto a terraced garden at the rear of the house.

The most interesting feature of the upper floor is the loggia around the courtyard. At the end of one of its wings is a small, baroque oratory. The drawing room contains some fresco paintings and a splendid collection of French console tables and Spanish paper baskets.

Although the house was built in the sixteenth century, extensive alterations were carried out during the seventeenth and nineteenth centuries, as was the case with most Sevillian houses.

The Marquis of Lozoya described the Palacio de Lebrija in the calle Cuna as the best paved house in the world. Its 580 square metres of Roman mosaic flooring certainly back up the claims of this statement. As well as the mosaics, the house contains Roman archaeological remains that were found in a property near the Roman ruins of Italica.

PALACIO DE LEBRIJA, SEVILLE A detail of the intricate stone carvings of the arcade.

Opposite PALACIO DE LEBRIJA The main courtyard is paved with an enormous mosaic representing the god Pan at its centre and other mythological scenes. Twenty-five circular forms are linked together with mosaic rope. It dates from the second century and was taken from a property near Itálica in 1914.

Right PALACIO DE LEBRIJA A view of the interior of the 'Glass Room', so-called because its large skylight occupies the whole ceiling.

Opposite PALACIO DE LEBRIJA The elaborate, Moorish tiled walls of the 'Glass Room' give onto the loggia at the back.

Below PALACIO DE LEBRIJA A view of the gallery, with its showcases of archaeological remains and collections of china and decorated cabinets.

Left PALACIO DE LEBRIJA The gallery on the upper floor is arranged around the main courtyard and leads to the various rooms and annexes. Portraits of the Counts of Lebrija and of the Marquises of Méritos hang from the walls.

PALACIO DE LEBRIJA The 'White Room' with a *Virgin and Child* attributed to Van Dyck over the fireplace and, over the sofa, a seventeenth-century painting from the School of Murillo representing Saints Justa and Rufina.

PALACIO DE LEBRIJA A portrait by Joaquín Sorolla (1863–1923) of the Countess of Lebrija, who was responsible for the considerable restorations carried out in the house; on either side are Chinese vases.

PALACIO DE LEBRIJA Fragments of Roman
sculptures and gravestones form part of the
collection.

PALACIO DE LEBRIJA Statues, capitals and fragments of mosaics, pedestals
and busts are displayed throughout the rooms on the lower floor.

Left PALACIO DE LEBRIJA The floors of this ground-floor room are paved
with geometric Roman mosaics. On the walls, archaeological remains
found near Itálica at the turn of the century are displayed.

Opposite PALACIO DE LEBRIJA One of the most important mosaics of the
house, depicting ocean life and dating from the first century AD, is
thought originally to have been part of a large fountain.

PALACIO DE LEBRIJA Red fabric covers the
walls of the library, where austere
Renaissance armchairs are combined with
the more baroque gilt ornamentation of
the showcases. A portrait of Federico
Sanchez Bedoya looks out over the room.

PALACIO DE LEBRIJA The Spanish dining room. The
ceiling is decorated with curious wooden star-shapes
with ceramic plates stuck to them.

PALACIO DE LEBRIJA A neo-
classical sculpture in one of
the rooms on the lower floor.

At the beginning of the century, Doña Regla Manjón, Countess of Lebrija, a learned lady and archaeology enthusiast, restored the house and added these impressive finds. Two hundred square metres of Roman paving discovered five metres deep at Santiponce are protected by iron railings and can be admired from the lovely sixteenth-century portico. The eighteenth-century tiled panels embellishing the entrance show allegorical motifs.

The floor of the loggia surrounding the main courtyard is of Roman porphyry marble and in its centre is the famous and vast (its sides are almost seven metres long) mosaic – found almost intact in 1914 in the olive groves of Los Palacios – representing Pan, in a central medallion, surrounded by scenes of Zeus's metamorphosis. Several other archaeological remains are exhibited in glass cases around the loggia.

The gallery leads onto a series of rooms also paved with mosaics, the most interesting being the *ochavado* room with its central fountain, the dance hall paved with Santiponce mosaics and the Medusa, Dionysius and Ganymedes rooms. These open onto secluded terraced gardens and courtyards in the traditional Sevillian style and feature a white, Italian marble fountain.

The present wide, three-flight staircase replaced the old one, which was much

PALACIO DE LEBRIJA A ceramic tile panel from the carriage entrance. The various panels represent the Continents, the Senses and the Fine Arts. This panel represents Asia.

narrower. It is decorated with sixteenth-century tiles from an abandoned convent and has a magnificent *artesonado* from the palace of Marchena, as well as a lovely Renaissance frieze in which the Ponce de León family coat-of-arms appears between busts of ladies and gentlemen crowned by a row of skulls. On the first floor, the mosaics are replaced by velvet draperies, tapestries and carpets. The glass-covered gallery around the courtyard contains showcases with collections of china and inlaid ivory and tortoiseshell writing-desks. The most interesting rooms are the dining room, the library and the sitting room, with their magnificent old red velvet draperies and their collections of furniture and paintings and a large Spanish knot carpet.

The Palacio de Niebla, or the house of the Lords of Sanlúcar, is the solitary and proud palace of the Guzmáns, the rebellious and powerful family which made its mark on Andalusia during eight hundred years and from whom the dukes of Medina Sidonia are descended. During all that time, the house was

CASA DE MEDINA SIDONIA The courtyard of Picadero, seen from the gallery of the house. The
Church of the Mercedes is seen beyond. The courtyard is the oldest remaining part of the house.

neither sold nor bought, but remained in the same family. They had moved to this old Arab citadel for military reasons, leaving their fortress in Niebla, and from here, they witnessed and participated in the main events that shaped the history of Andalusia and of Spain. Columbus stayed in the house before setting out for America; several kings, including Enrique IV, Pedro I and Felipe IV also slept here. Goya made sketches here and even Quevedo and the famous Duchess of Alba, who was also Duchess of Medina Sidonia, were guests here.

Guzmán el Bueno, after being made a lord of Sanlúcar in 1296 for his feats against the Arabs, was the first owner, and he reconstructed the small military fortress, an old eleventh-century, Moorish citadel. The church of the 'O', adjoining the palace, was built in the fourteenth century by a descendent of his, Doña Leonor de la Cerda y de Guzmán.

The Guzmáns were a family with strong loyalties, who involved themselves in fierce confrontations with the established powers, earning them the highest honours but also the most severe punishments. The fourth Lord of Sanlúcar was granted the Countship of Niebla when he married Beatriz, an illegitimate daughter of King Enrique de Trastamara; their son died in an attempt to conquer Gibraltar and another of their descendants was burnt at the stake by the Inquisition. The third Duke of Medina Sidonia, an alchemist, was also punished by the Holy Office and in the nineteenth century, yet another had his house and lands confiscated for being a Carlist. The Duchy of Medina Sidonia was granted to the third Count of Niebla in 1435 and is currently one of the oldest surviving dukedoms in Spain.

New buildings and lands were gradually annexed to the medieval fortress, which grew into a large, irregular estate. By the sixteenth century, Sanlúcar was the main residence of the Dukes of Medina Sidonia, who carried out works of restoration and embellishment to provide the whole property with a certain overall coherence. Reconstruction proceeded continuously from 1528 to 1641, when the second Duke was banished from Andalusia and confined to the castle of Coca.

Attempts were made to remodel the exteriors by building a traditional courtyard and by landscaping a nearby wood with terraces and avenues; exotic animals, fruit trees and rare plants were added, as well as statues, paintings, fountains and cascades. Wells and tanks were required to supply the garden with water and an Italian engineer called Leudovico, expert in aquatic devices, was commissioned to channel the water through lead pipes. At the bottom of the garden, there was an artificial grotto decorated with paintings that led to a maze of cascades and canals. It must have been a beautiful garden, more Italian in style than traditionally Andalusian, and only a small part of it has survived.

The interior has been changed over the centuries in a series of alterations influenced by prevailing fashions or by the family's requirements, with mixed results. For example, a magnificent, Mudéjar, scissor-design ceiling in one of the rooms was covered by baroque plaster reliefs in 1640. The mid-fifteenth-century column

Opposite CASA DE MEDINA SIDONIA
The Duke's bedroom, with its
elaborate seventeenth-century
Florentine bed with ivory and
mother-of-pearl inlays, repeated on
the bedside tables.

Right CASA DE MEDINA SIDONIA
The extraordinarily comprehensive
archives of the ducal house.

CASA DE MEDINA SIDONIA The dining
room has a Spanish table and
eighteenth-century Cordoban chairs.
The Flemish tapestry depicting a
religious theme dates from the
seventeenth-century and an altar
front from the Church of the
Mercedes can be seen over the door.

room was partitioned when closing an open loggia that joined two wings of the original building. The staircase and garden colonnade were built during the seventeenth century and the lovely Tarifa tiles on the living room fireplace were covered with stuccos and a pompous plaster coat-of-arms in the nineteenth century. During the sixteenth century, the walls displayed mural paintings and frescos that were covered a century later by tapestries and pictures. They soon grew into a significant collection which, together with the rich furniture and valuable china, gradually gave this unusual property its right to be called a palace.

Towards the middle of the seventeenth century, the King ordered the Dukes to move to Valladolid and the house and garden were left unattended. The property continued deteriorating until it was converted into a hospital during the war of Independence. Later, when the Dukes were accused of being Carlists and their possessions confiscated, first a gardener, then a market gardener and finally a stockman took over the building, the last using it as granary and depot. On their return from exile in 1847, the Dukes again settled in the mansion and started a series of typical, nineteenth-century, clearly French-inspired restoration works. The original clay floors were replaced by slabs of Genoese and Sevillian marble; French fireplaces, paintings and tapestries were added.

The palace is not easily classified, as it belongs to a succession of periods and styles, each one of which left its mark. Moorish, Mudéjar, Gothic or baroque remains appear in corners throughout the house and in areas such as the small *covachas*, stalls that had once formed an Arab market, the *picadero*, the ambassadors' room, the columned loggia and in some of the gardens, that are now merely ruins but still contain some species of exceptional interest. Such diversity comes together, however, in an overall spirit that is uniquely Andalusian.

The palace archives are one of the greatest treasures of the house and the present Duchess herself catalogued, studied and organized their priceless documents: 6,300 bundles of papers, some of which contain more than five hundred documents. The oldest date back to the twelfth century and come from León. The Andalusian archive dates to the thirteenth century and consists of two parts, one corresponding to the Medina Sidonia family and the other to the Fajardo family. The history of Sanlúcar appears in unpublished form in numerous documents describing wars and campaigns or referring to Columbus's voyages and his relationship with this ducal house.

GRANADA

We have come to the last of the four kingdoms that formed Andalusia. It was in Granada that the Arabs stayed longest and they converted it into a beautiful, rich and self-sufficient city which, after the *Reconquista*, was the true source of the Renaissance style in Andalusia.

Granada has a different spirit to all the cities we have described, perhaps due to its position, surrounded by mountains - the snow-capped peaks of Sierra

CASA DE MEDINA SIDONIA Moorish twelfth- and thirteenth-century arches around the courtyard.

Opposite CASA DE MEDINA SIDONIA A view of the 'Column Room', clearly showing the sixteenth-century Triana wall tiles and the fireplace. The large coat-of-arms above it dates from work done in the nineteenth century. The floor is covered with Andalusian clay tiles.

Opposite CASA DEL MARQUÉS DE SALVATIERRA
The bright and sunny drawing room acts as a
portrait gallery.

Nevada, which turn pink when sprinkled with the desert sand blown in on the winds from the Sahara. The Arabs transformed the valley into a fertile market garden: almost 600,000 acres of land with over thirty water mills and three hundred farms. When the Empire crumbled, Granada became independent and reached its apotheosis with the dynasty of the Nasrids, who made it their capital city.

This dynasty built the Medinat Al Hambra, the jewel of Granada and of all Andalusia. The Moorish Kings paid annual tributes to, and pacted with, the Christian Kings and their relationship was more one of allies than of natural enemies. Thus, for example, they helped Fernando, 'the Saint', to conquer Seville and later supplied Pedro I with the masons he required to build the Reales Alcázares.

CASA DEL MARQUÉS DE SALVATIERRA The
Nasrid garden is on two levels and looks over
the city walls.

To some extent, this ambiguity allowed them to outlive the other Arab kingdoms in the peninsula and to house Muslims fleeing from elsewhere in the region within their city walls. And while Cordoba looked to Europe for its splendid buildings, Granada turned in on its own Moorish traditions.

There is a legend that blames the Arab invasion of the peninsula on an offence committed against a woman: the daughter of a powerful lord of the Atlas was seduced and dishonoured by Rodrigo. Another legend lays the blame of the end of the Arab reign of Granada on the quarrels between two royal ladies: Zoraya, a captive Christian with whom King Muley Hassan fell in love and his lawful wife, Aïsha, whom he disowned. Years later, one of Hassan's sons, Boabdil, dethroned his father and became the last King of Granada, a weak monarch who cried when he handed the keys of paradise to his enemies, the Catholic sovereigns, while his mother reproached him for 'shedding tears like a woman for what you were unable to defend as a man'.

After the *Reconquista*, the first master masons gradually arrived in the city. Architects such as García de Prados or Joaquin Marquina started making a name for themselves until, in 1527, Pedro Machuca began building the Palacio de Carlos V in the Alhambra. Diego de Siloé arrived from Naples in 1528 to complete the church of San Jerónimo and to work on the cathedral and the church of the Saviour. He participated in the construction of numerous religious buildings; his works of civil architecture were far less abundant, the most noteworthy being the Palacio de la Chancilleria (1546) and the Casa de los Miradores.

Ronda also belonged to the kingdom of Granada. It is a mysterious city whose position and surrounding landscape have never failed to fascinate visitors. The river Guadalquivir divided the city into Arab and Christian parts, and in the latter the house of the Marquises of Salvatierra was built, in a privileged position on the gorge surrounding the city and on the original Arab walls.

After the city was taken in 1485, the houses that had belonged to the Muslims were shared out among the conquerors' families. Don Vasco de Salvatierra, a knight from Extremadura, arrived in Ronda with the conquering forces and founded a lineage in the town. His sixteenth-century mansion, built on the remains of a Muslim palace, was altered during the eighteenth century. The façade is sober, except for the richly-carved entrance arch crowned by the family coat-of-arms. It has a lovely courtyard surrounded by irregular-shaped columns. The imperial staircase, made with three different coloured marbles – red from Cabra, white from Estepa and black from Granada – is topped by a dome and coat-of-arms. The house also has a small, very secluded baroque oratory, interesting tiles in the dining room and in some other rooms, as well as a collection of old china and beautiful plasterwork in the sitting room.

The terraced garden, with views over the city walls, is typical of the Granada-Nasrid style. From this lovely, secluded corner, one of the most impressive views of the Ronda gorge is enhanced by the climbing wysteria, jasmine and roses which cover the building's walls.

THE BAROQUE STYLE

THE EUROPEAN BAROQUE STYLE was really forged during the course of the seventeenth century, a hundred years before the Andalusian baroque palaces were built. This was an unsettled time for Spain, full of contradictions; it was the century of Calderonian honour and crooked Monipodio, of Valdés Leal and the buying of noble titles, of Gracián and Góngara, of Zurbarán, Rubens and Quevedo, a character considered by all to be a naïve soul with a wicked tongue. It was a century when Spain, in spite of still being the greatest and richest Empire in the world, was feeling deeply wounded by the vicissitudes of fate. The kingdom was stifled by its financial obligations and by its incapacity to control them, to the extent that the King's daily preoccupation became one of how to pay for his own meals and clothes.

Once again, Spanish society heralded a new century accompanied by the cruel din of an expulsion, this time of the Arabs. The process took a long time and in many ways was forced on the country by the Church. Three hundred thousand Mudéjares (Christians living in those parts of Spain which were ruled by Muslims), or double and even triple that number, depending on the source, had to abandon the country, leaving the fertile lands of Granada, Aragon, Valencia and Murcia unattended. The region of Granada suffered the most and took more than a century to recover.

Castile, once again, became depopulated. Many Castilians fled to America in search of fortune and their cities became impoverished because the noblemen followed the King and Court, by then established in the Palacio del Buen Retiro in Madrid. To make things worse, two plagues broke out (in 1648 and 1653), particularly disastrously in Andalusia, and the Spanish population was reduced to eight million.

Page 132 CASA DE CAMPO REAL, JEREZ DE LA FRONTERA The courtyard was inspired by Italian Renaissance models, with its stone ovals in the arcades representing the Virtues and two busts of the founders of the house.

Neither the aristocracy nor the Church was immune to the crisis. Religion became the only consolation of a disappointed country that, when faced with its sombre and disconcerting future, turned obstinately to spiritualism and scorned all knowledge and humanism. It could not accept that as the most powerful kingdom in the world it was incapable of destroying its enemies, who instead multiplied and humiliated it. Only in the unearthly world could there be an explanation for the social cataclysm that had attacked the Spanish kingdoms. This way of thinking was the basis for the twisted and lacerating conscience of a nation that blamed itself for the ill-fated events which it faced. Increasing numbers of people entered the Church and some cities took in more clerics than laymen.

And the aristocracy also increased in number. The King and his chancellors were compelled to sell noble titles to the gentry, who wanted them at any price. A title was desirable for a number of reasons: the aristocracy was exempt from all taxes; a title was an essential requirement for holding any state or military rank, the only professions allowed to a gentleman; and, lastly, the nobility enjoyed almost full immunity before the Inquisition. They gave financial support to the Church, to the measure of their rank, by keeping private chaplains, making enormous donations and alms and paying for grand, local religious ceremonies. The aristocracy prided itself on what was perhaps the last legacy of their feudal past: noblemen live or should live on private income as proof of their status, without practising any profession, except by royal assignment.

THE SEVILLIAN MANOR HOUSE

During the seventeenth century, Seville had become a metropolis with motley crowds filling its streets and products from all over the world in its shops and on its market stalls. Money flowed freely and merchants from all over Europe met in the port, where galleons arrived regularly loaded with precious wood, dyes, fruits and medicinal roots, exotic birds and beasts and, above all, American silver and gold.

Under the shelter of this busy new city, houses were built gradually to replace the Moorish ones. Along the narrow, winding streets, a new type of house and a more modern city was taking shape. The owners, proud of their lineage, wanted their new houses to be like palaces and the buildings were certainly more ostentatious than the Moorish residences. Seville filled up with these mansions, especially in the districts of San Andrés and the Arenal. They were the homes of the *hijosdalgos*, or *hidalgos*, the foreign and Castilian merchants, and of some noblemen who, whilst they possessed properties in the kingdom, were not powerful enough to build great palaces.

The structure of the baroque houses was similar to those built during the Renaissance. Their owners were not affluent enough to build *apeaderos*, but invented the *casapuerta*, a spacious and well-lit lobby that nevertheless denoted the owner's social standing. This entrance area was elaborately decorated, often panelled with brightly-coloured, Arcadian picture tiles. A lantern hanging from the ceiling gave the room a Moorish feel, with its red and green stained-glass pieces. The staircase next to the *casapuerta* had marble steps and a colourful, tiled hand-guard.

By this stage of building patterns, it was possible to enter the courtyard directly, as the doors faced each other, allowing a view of the patio from the street through a latticed grill. The religious order to keep the doors of a Moorish house open dictated this new arrangement, where the front grill, acting as door, allowed a view inside the house while still protecting it from outsiders. The courtyard, as usual, was the place of honour. It had barrel or horseshoe arches, preferably with Tuscan capitals on granite columns. A central fountain was popular, although in some cases a marble or even tiled basin was set in the wall.

The most sumptuous houses built an oratory or shrine dedicated to the household's patron saint in the courtyard arcade, flanked by classical columns

CASA DE LAS COLUMNAS, ANTEQUERA The covered entrance hall and the carriage entrance are separated by a gate. A lovely wire and glass lantern hangs from the ceiling.

and with silver candle-holders. The limewashed façades were distinguished by stone foundation plinths highlighted with paint or decorative tiles.

When comparing this seventeenth-century construction with that of the old Moorish house, its spaciousness is the most obvious difference. These were the residences of wealthy families and occupied the same ground space as two or three Arab houses. They were designed for knights or merchants with recently-bought titles of nobility – a social group that was more common in Seville than in any other city, largely because of the fabulous business opportunities offered by its position as customs port of the riches from America. Such houses are far from being examples of popular architecture, as they were expressly designed for the wealthy and their style was influenced by the Renaissance palace rather than by the Moorish residence. But for several reasons – their great number, their common features and their almost simultaneous construction – they can be fully identified as representative of the city of Seville. In form, they successfully combined a demonstration of social rank with an arrangement for efficient day-to-day life, and their architecture was respected by the Sevillians for almost two centuries. They are the full expression of the unique Sevillian baroque architectural style, with their tiled surfaces, carved wooden ceilings and ornamental railings.

THE ANDALUSIAN BAROQUE PALACE

A true Andalusian baroque style of palace architecture appeared in Seville about fifty or sixty years later than the more conventional, large baroque houses commissioned by the new aristocracy. These palaces were scattered throughout what was then the kingdom of Seville, in Écija, Estepa, Carmona or Jerez de la Frontera, as well as in Seville itself. The Court capital was by then Madrid, which is where the grandees built their Court residences.

The lords of the baroque Andalusian palace built large, rambling houses close to their lands, either within the towns or on their country estates or in nearby villages. This aristocracy, who gradually became related by marriage to the grandees of Spain, or were descended from lesser, secondary branches, had no direct link with the old Castilian families. But the baroque palaces, in spite of being founded in this new Age of Enlightenment, were still built in the spirit of the feudal fortresses. They were equally lavish, used the same grand classical symbolism and were again built far from the Court capital, Madrid. This did not, of course, prevent the Andalusian aristocracy from having residences in Madrid, Seville or Cordoba as well as outside the cities; on the contrary, as soon as they ensured their status and incomes, members of this aristocracy first built a house near their estates and then another near the Court.

Although the architectural structure of the new palaces was based on that of the great Renaissance palaces, it nevertheless displayed a number of decorative variations. All the new palaces were built with grand doorways, with the former, simple ornamentation replaced by baroque stonework reaching over

Opposite CASA DE LOS DUQUES DE OSUNA, SEVILLE The luxuriant courtyard of the Casa de los Duques de Osuna is one of the most beautiful in Seville. A summer dining room is protected from the heat by the white curtains hung from the pillars.

both floors. The façades were no longer blind walls separating the *apeaderos* from the street, but had become, like those of the palaces of Úbeda, one of the houses' main walls. The façades might be limewashed, with simple openings covered with ornamental ironwork, but in many cases they were more elaborate. The palace of Cerverales in Estepa, for example, has a carved stone façade; the Palacio Benamejí in Écija has a brickwork front; and the palace of Peñaflor, also in Écija, boasts a continuous balcony. But the only embellishment on the façade of the Domecqs' palace in Jerez is the entrance arch, the rest being limewashed wall.

The carriage entrance was no longer an independent yard, but either ceased to be built or was integrated into the main building behind the façade in the form of an ante-courtyard, smaller than the original *picadero*. The stables and coach

PALACIO DE PEÑAFLOR, ÉCIJA This is
the most famous balcony in Écija,
running fifty-six metres along the
whole façade of the palace. It is
decorated with frescos depicting
architectural elements and
landscapes.

houses were also included in the ground-floor plan of the building and not as independent annexes.

The courtyard still maintained its function of grand reception area with the whole house organized around it. But the double-porticoed loggia was no longer considered essential and normally there was only a corridor on the lower floor. The upper-floor gallery looked over the courtyard through arched or flat openings. In some cases, the staircase was now in a different position and dominated the courtyard, rather than rising from one side of it.

The design of the gardens also underwent changes and became less important in the architectural scheme. During the baroque period, the classical symbolism that had made the gardens of the Renaissance places of educational mysticism was no longer a consideration. Instead, the gardens became secondary and optional features that depended on the space available or on the owners' preferences.

CASA DE LOS CONDES DE SANTA COLOMA, SEVILLE A detail of a door of a painted and gilded writing-desk.

Opposite PALACIO DE PEÑAFLOR This typically baroque architectural arrangement has the double staircase rising from the entrance hall of triple arches.

One of the most splendid and clearest examples of the Sevillian baroque *casa-palacio*, with all its characteristic features, is the house of the Bucarelli, or Palacio de los Condes de Santa Coloma, in the calle Santa Clara. It was commissioned in 1780 by Don Antonio Bucarelli, Marquis of Villahermosa, ancestor of the Santa Coloma family, who originally came from Florence. It is a two-storied building, looking over three streets. The long main façade is divided by windows separated by pilasters on each floor. The magnificent doorway rises the whole height of the building and is richly adorned with pediments, mouldings and Corinthian pilasters. The cornice above the entrance holds up a balcony decorated with finials and the family coat-of-arms.

The porch opens onto a semi-covered carriage entrance, or *casapuerta*, with English-style stables on the right. The loggia half covering the *apeadero* leads to the main courtyard off one of its corners. The courtyard has arches on all four sides and on both floors. The lower-floor arches are semi-circular, with marble columns, and are decorated with vellum-like bricks, rather like those in the courtyard of the Hospital de los Venerables. The upper-floor arches are closed, with balconies. As well as the entrance area and main courtyard, the house has three more courtyards and a large garden on the other side of a lovely colonnade around one of the smaller courtyards.

The two-flight, vaulted staircase rises from one of the main courtyard fronts and leads to the first floor, where the main rooms of the house are situated. The drawing rooms, dining room, the glass-covered gallery and the bedrooms still have their seventeenth-century Sevillian tiles. There was also a chapel, now converted into a living room.

In spite of its having undergone alterations, the house, which is one of the most handsome in Seville, is a well preserved example of the original layout of a late eighteenth-century *casa-palacio*.

Another interesting example of Sevillian baroque is the Casa de Ibarra in the calle Bailén. The house of the Duchess of Osuna was built in the seventeenth century, and in spite of numerous alterations, several details of its original architecture have survived. Its architect was Admiral López Pintado. An adjoining building was added on later. The basic structure of the house has been respected and the original ornamental ironwork, floors and railings can still be seen, along with a large number of paintings, tapestries, chinawares and furniture. In addition to all these treasures, the palace has one of the most beautiful courtyards in the city.

CASA DE LOS CONDES DE SANTA COLOMA
A view through the carriage entrance,
looking into the main courtyard.

Opposite CASA DE LOS CONDES DE SANTA COLOMA A detail from one of the tapestries hanging in the dining room.

CASA DE LOS CONDES DE SANTA COLOMA The dining room is furnished with an English table and chairs upholstered in red velvet. A Chinese lacquer screen partitions off the next room.

ESTEPA

The Palacio del Marqués de Cerverales is the most important civil building in Estepa. It was completed in 1756 by the vicar Don Manuel Bejarano y Fonseca, who leased it to his nephew, the first Marquis of Cerverales, Don Manuel Díaz Fonseca. The palace is currently the residence of his descendants and is in an excellent state of conservation.

The palace is particularly interesting, as it is linked to the adjoining Church of the Asunción through a portico protected by lattice-work. There is also a corridor leading to a private chapel where four members of the family are buried.

CASA DE MOINET IBARRA, SEVILLE A detail of one of the arches, with its austerely-carved capital.

Opposite CASA DE MOINET IBARRA In the formal courtyard, with its central fountain and marble columns, the walls are limewashed in a stunning red ochre.

CASA DE MOINET IBARRA The upper gallery gives onto the main rooms of the house.

The chapel is a good example of religious Andalusian baroque and is separated from the rest of the church by an iron grating.

The façade is decorated with a stone fascia on both floors, similar to styles used at Úbeda. The lower section contains four openings which reach ground level and are flanked by pilasters, supporting a cornice on which the upper openings rest, forming an almost neo-classical geometrical structure. The large upper windows are crowned by split pediments with a kind of stone lantern at the open apex. The façade is topped by a simple, shallow cornice with a central allegorical figure jutting out above the building's façade over the porch, which itself spans both floors. The columns support genuinely baroque capitals. Three carved mermaids hold up the central balcony.

The courtyard has a central fountain and double arcade with barrel arches. The lower portico is held up by stone shafts with Tuscan capitals, while the upper one is obscured, converting the columns into pilasters. In the middle of the old arch curve, simple balcony-like openings have been made to let light into the corridor and the old loggia. The tiling in the courtyard is interesting, and in each corner there is a carved *fleur-de-lis* as token of the owners' gratitude and loyalty to the new Bourbon dynasty which had granted them their title.

CARMONA

This walled town is situated not far from Seville and was already thriving when the Phoenician traders arrived. It was later inhabited by the Carthaginians, then by the Romans, and it had also been an independent Muslim kingdom.

The town was an impenetrable fortress that nobody had managed to take by siege. Several kings had lived in its castle – Pedro of Castile, for example, converted it into a sumptuous residence for himself and some of his mistresses – although it also constituted a sinister prison where tragic events took place. After the earthquake of 1508, the castle was abandoned and fell into ruins.

The mixture of customs and religions that flourished side by side in the town resulted in a spirit of mutual tolerance and in a particular architectural style that was respected in the successive restorations of buildings and streets, and which has survived in the town to the present day. The owners of large, landed

CASA DE LOS MARQUESES DE CERVERALES A striking portrait of Don Manuel de Reina y Juarez de Negrin, sixth Marquis of Cerverales, painted in a naïve style.

Right CASA DE LOS MARQUESES DE CERVERALES The 'Alphonsine Room', with its richly-brocaded suite of chairs.

Opposite CASA DE LOS MARQUESES DE CERVERALES The 'Baroque Room' is named after the elaborate console-table and mirror on the left; the rest of the furnishings are Isabelline.

Opposite CASA DE LOS MARQUESES DE CERVERALES A baroque campaign oratory, made in 1754, with its folding doors closed.

Right CASA DE LOS MARQUESES DE CERVERALES The open doors reveal the richly-gilded altarpiece with a contrasting, modest terracotta figure of Christ on the cross.

CASA DE LOS MARQUESES DE CERVERALES A detail of the altarpiece, showing the full wealth and variety of the craftsmanship employed in its making.

Opposite CASA DE LOS MARQUESES DE CERVERALES The charming courtyard, with its pots of roses and geraniums, is surrounded by a double arcade of barrel arches supported by columns on the lower level and pilasters on the upper floor.

CASA DE LOS MARQUESES DE CALTOJAR, CARMONA An intimate, brick-paved room, now used as the house's administrative office.

CASA DE LOS MARQUESES DE CALTOJAR The Mudéjar courtyard, with its octagonal columns and original cobbled paving (little survives in Carmona) is one of the oldest parts of the house and used to be a farm building.

Opposite CASA DE LOS MARQUESES DE CALTOJAR A view of the galleried stables of the house.

properties in the surrounding fertile valley built their mansions in the town. Many of these date from the sixteenth century, although almost all were altered in the eighteenth and even in the nineteenth centuries.

Situated in the highest part of the town is the house of the Marquises of Caltojar. Like most Carmona houses, its walls are limewashed down to ground level and it is hardly distinguishable from its neighbours; only a great wooden door shows that this must be a grand mansion. Its interior is bathed in a special light and creates an atmosphere where time seems to have stood still. The house has, in fact, belonged to the same family since it was built. The oldest parts – some courtyards and passageways on the ground floor – date back to the time of the Arab occupation. The palace consists of two houses, the main building for the noble household and the *casa de labor* that was used to house all the property's farm equipment and administrative offices. Today, both houses are connected. It also has seven courtyards and stables that were once a granary. Each of the seven courtyards had a different function. One of them still has its original Mudéjar octagonal brick columns and cobbled floors, amongst the few to have survived intact in the city.

Opposite CASA DE LOS MARQUESES DE CALTOJAR
The living room in the main house is heavily
decorated in nineteenth-century French style, with
striped wallpaper and pink satin upholstery.

CASA DE LOS MARQUESES DE CALTOJAR Another richly-decorated
room has imitation silk wallpaper and red damask upholstery and
curtains. The sofa and pedestal table are Isabelline, and the walls
are hung with a collection of miniatures and religious paintings.

Opposite CASA DE LASSO DE LA VEGA,
CARMONA The courtyard now boasts a
swimming pool, seen here from one of the
landscaped gardens, with flower beds and
earth paths.

The main house was built later than the farm building; documents record 1716 as the year of its construction. The primary rooms are laid out in the traditional pattern for summer and winter use. The drawing rooms on the upper floor show a clear nineteenth-century French influence, as do many in the town, as a result of its proximity to Seville, where French fashions prevailed. The rooms are full of carpets, furniture, draperies and painted wallpaper, all brought from France and preserved in exquisite condition.

The house that had belonged to the Lasso de la Vega family in the same town was recently converted into a successful hotel, but still retains the elements characteristic of Carmona mansions. Although its origins date back to before the sixteenth century, with Mudéjar remains, it underwent so many alterations during subsequent centuries that it appears not as a Renaissance house but as a clear example of the transition to the baroque style.

The property includes a series of annexes around a central courtyard, once a loggia, where a beautiful marble colonnade was discovered during recent

CASA DE LASSO DE LA VEGA A lovely fountain basin in a small yard. The tiling has been done with remains of ceramic strips and old skirtings from the house.

CASA DE LASSO DE LA VEGA The main balcony over the door of the house, with the family coat-of-arms below.

Opposite CASA DE LASSO DE LA VEGA The staircase, with a double arch, is beautifully limewashed in shades of terracotta.

restoration works. The upper gallery has three covered sides and a fourth uncovered, as in the Mudéjar palaces of Dueñas and Pilatos; other indications that it had once been a Mudéjar palace are its irregular ground-plan and typical arrangement of asymmetrical inner courtyards.

During the seventeenth century, the palace was extensively adapted to the Italian fashion prevailing in Seville. The front door and the arched loggia, with its three rows of columns, were built at that time. The dance hall was built in the eighteenth century by pulling down partitions and walls to give the room a new configuration.

The most recent alterations, supervised by Marta Medina, have attempted to restore the original appearance of the house. Clay tiles cover the floors and the façade has been painted in the traditional Andalusian manner with limewash and pigments, as was the custom for centuries. Local craftsmen have restored the tiles and woodwork, although the colours of the walls and ceilings are not true to the original design and many of the tapestries and furniture are of English origin.

ÉCIJA

Opposite CASA DE LASSO DE LA VEGA The living room cum library acts as a print room for a large collection.

This town is a baroque gem, the 'city of the thousand towers', known as the Toledo of the south. It is also famous for its woodwork, its sweetmeats and its main square, popularly known as *el Salón*. Hidden among its streets are the baroque palaces to which the town owes its fame.

The palace of Peñaflor has the date 1726 carved on its façade. The building has two stories and a corner doorway, instead of one centring the whole façade. A continuous fifty-nine metre long balcony is the palace's most distinctive symbol, dominating the façade and relegating the great door to the status of a secondary feature. On the wall of the balcony, some unusual *trompe-l'oeil* architectural paintings hide the simplicity of the brick surface.

The doorway is fairly simple, flanked by two columns on pedestals with Tuscan capitals. The entrance supports a split, curved pediment (similar to those on the palace of Cerverales) containing the balcony, flanked by the inevitable classical columns of the period and topped with the family coat-of-arms on its lintel. A turret rises above the attic at the left-hand corner of the façade.

The porch opens onto an *apeadero* fully integrated into the building, containing an interesting, carved stone trough. To the left is the *casa-puerta* and facing this a staircase presided over by the Virgin of the Rosary, which is perhaps the most interesting feature of the whole entrance area. Designed to allow direct access to the entrances, the stairs end in two separate flights and have a triple arcade of very similar workmanship to that of the staircase at the palace of Benamejí. It is decorated with plasterwork and crowned with a frescoed dome.

The courtyard is considered the most beautiful in Écija. It is surrounded by a double loggia of marble columns with a baroque fountain at its centre. The frieze, composed of black Cordoba marble, pinkish Cabra marble and Lanjarón agate, is particularly striking. A collection of agate and gilt-wood cornucopias add to the courtyard's elegance. The upper floors contain coffered Renaissance ceilings formed by octagonal panels.

The Palacio Benamejí was designed by the Écija-born architect Pablo Gutiérrez. Two watch-towers, or *miradores*, rise above the attic on either side. A story is told about these towers. Carlos III granted Don Fadrique de Benuy, Marquis of Benamejí, the right to build one tower, whilst the Marquis erected the second one for his own convenience. When the King stayed at the palace on his return from a visit to Seville, he called the Marquis's attention to the existence of the double *mirador* and reprimanded him because he had only ordered the construction of one. The crafty Marquis replied that his title gave him the right to the other; luckily the King was amused by his impudence.

The palace is another of the town's beautiful baroque buildings. There are no windows on the ground floor section of the façade, but the upper floor has ten, five on either side of the large doorway of rich stonework framed by columns, pedestals, lintels and coats-of-arms – without doubt the most impressive

PALACIO DE PEÑAFLOR A view up into the staircase dome, decorated with intricate plasterwork.

Opposite PALACIO DE PEÑAFLOR The staircase is dominated by a Sevillian painting of the *Virgin of the Rosary*, framed by elaborate plasterwork and set against a decorative dome.

in Écija. Behind the doorway are the features common to all palaces of baroque design: the *casapuerta*, with the stables on the right, and, at the end of the carriage entrance facing the front doorway, the staircase. This is a magnificent construction with three, double-rise, foiled arches (again, similar to the one at Peñaflor) enclosing a central passageway to the great courtyard. The central arch rests on double, streaked marble columns with Tuscan capitals, below an enormous arch supporting a balcony, in an overall arrangement which appears like a second front entrance.

The main courtyard is formed by a double gallery with various different arches: the upper one has segmented arches, like those at Dueñas and the lower one has barrel arches, all supported by columns. In the centre of the courtyard is a fountain carved in marble and stone. The right wing of the palace opens onto a garden.

There are no treasures to be seen inside the mansion, because in 1906 it was sold by the last descendants of Don Fadrique to the city authorities to be converted into military headquarters.

The house of the Dukes of Almenara Alta in the calle de los Mármoles is another superb palace. Its bare brick façade has an original carved stone doorway of a very simple baroque design, crowned by a niche containing a statue of the Virgin de la Soledad. Its beautiful and well cared-for interior again contains a monumental staircase and also some splendid doors, many of which are polychrome or painted with allegorical motifs. There is a Mudéjar courtyard and lovely, well-kept gardens and recent improvements have been carried out on the whole estate.

CADIZ

A very busy sea-port, Cadiz experienced a remarkable economic expansion in the eighteenth century. By 1717, it held the monopoly of trade with America that had until then been Seville's privilege. In spite of the city being surrounded by defensive walls, important buildings were erected and a development plan was designed to modernize the city with avenues and houses. These included the famous *miradores*, in an architectural style that also appeared in Puerto de Santa Maria at this time. These watch-towers raised on the flat roofs were used to observe the movements of the ships in the bay, and although they originally date back to the Middle Ages, the versions built in the seventeenth century, and even more extensively in the eighteenth century, featured a wide variety of finials, forms and finishes.

Opposite PALACIO DE BENAMEJÍ, ÉCIJA The two-flight imperial staircase has grand, foiled arches. The central arch leads to the main courtyard and is crowned by a large dome.

PALACIO DE BENAMEJÍ Carved red marble columns on the entrance arch depict grotesque masks and drapery.

PALACIO DE LOS DUQUES DE ALMENARA ALTA, ÉCIJA

An extraordinary little Sevillian baroque

sculpture of a sleeping infant Jesus.

Opposite PALACIO DE LOS DUQUES DE ALMENARA ALTA

The 'Octagonal Room', with its spectacular ceiling

and painted cornice mouldings.

PALACIO DE LOS DUQUES DE ALMENARA ALTA

A view of the garden front of the palace
from the rose garden. A Roman milestone
in the foreground is now topped with an
iron cross.

PALACIO DE LOS DUQUES DE ALMENARA ALTA

The stables have been beautifully restored.

PALACIO DE LOS DUQUES DE ALMENARA ALTA

This door is painted with a very lively

Annunciation scene.

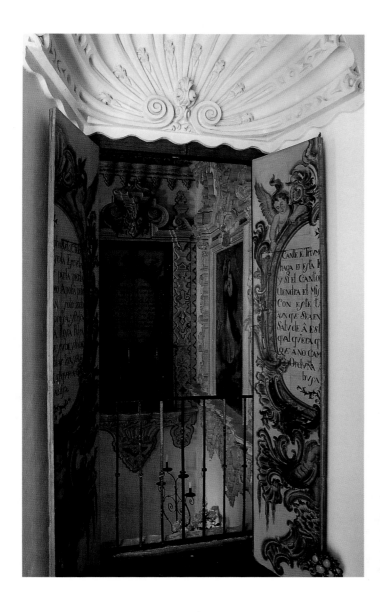

PALACIO DE LOS DUQUES DE ALMENARA ALTA
The painted panels of the balcony doors overlook the staircase.

Opposite PALACIO DE LOS DUQUES DE ALMENARA ALTA The staircase is hung with an image of the *Assumption*. Beneath is a gilt jardinière.

PALACIO DE LOS DUQUES DE ALMENARA ALTA A detail of the paintings on the doors of the balcony, depicting allegorical interpretations of the elements – here, Air and Fire.

Opposite PALACIO DEL MARQUÉS DE MONTANA, JEREZ DE LA FRONTERA The baroque staircase, with stone and red marble columns, is of grand proportions. The palace now houses the Domecq wine cellars.

JEREZ DE LA FRONTERA

Cadiz may have its palaces, but grand mansions proliferate in Jerez de la Frontera. The former Casa de Montana, today known as Palacio de Domecq, is one of the town's landmarks. It was built between 1775 and 1778 by the first Marquis of Montana, Don Antonio Cabezas de Aranda y Guzmán. Later, it was bought by the famous wine-producing family of French origin, today the Marquises of Domecq, hence its current name. The family had come from Bearn in Navarre, France, at the end of the eighteenth century to take possession of some vineyards near Jerez.

The palace is a symbol of Jerez's past greatness and economic expansion. The Marquis of Montana had certain difficulties with the building guild when he starting constructing his palace, because the plot was a flat piece of land the young aristocratic men of Jerez used for recreation. Carlos III reigned at the time and he applied strict town planning regulations. The difficulties were finally solved and the palace was built, according to a baroque design, by the Sevillian architect, Don Antonio Matias de Figueroa.

In contrast to the simplicity of the façade's wall surface, the baroque decoration is all concentrated on the doorway, made with stone from Puerto de Santa María. It has pilasters and classical columns and its highly-ornate carvings are centred on a large balcony, framed by pilasters at the corners. The whole quadrangular façade is influenced by the stonework of religious buildings of the period. It is arranged in two sections, separated by an *entresuelo* housing administrative and service areas, with a lower floor forming the attic. The surface consists of solid, limewashed areas with simple bay windows displaying fine ornamental ironwork, which is protected by dust-guards. The courtyard arches form an interesting, fully baroque structure, with the same motifs repeated in the upper-floor loggia, which has a very unusual type of column, that could be described as bulbous.

The staircase displays another typically baroque feature: the use of reddish marble with very elaborately carved vegetable motifs, with a triple arcade over groups of four columns. The stairs end on the second floor, which is the main floor of the house, but because of the added *entresuelo*, they extend far further than in any other building of the period.

The Casa de Campo Real, or palace of the Zurita family, situated in the historical centre of Jerez, is one of the city's oldest houses. After Jerez was reconquered in 1264, Alfonso X granted the plot to the Benavente y Cabeza de Vaca family, in whose hands it has remained right to the present day, that is, for over seven hundred years.

The house has undergone several alterations over the centuries. Its general architecture is Renaissance, with an Italian-style courtyard and splendid marble staircase. The courtyard arcades still have their stone mouldings representing the Virtues and other ideal accomplishments of the period, and another two medallions with busts of the founders can still be seen on its main front.

PALACIO DEL MARQUÉS DE MONTANA A view
of the courtyard and upper gallery, with
stone pilasters between the balconies.

Opposite CASA DE CAMPO REAL The well-
tended 'old' garden is built on two levels,
with stone steps and statues, parterres and
earth paths.

But the sixteenth-century façade was modified during the works carried
out in 1782 to give it a more imposing appearance. A Jerez architect, Don José de
Vargas, built the new façade in eighteenth-century neo-classical style, with an
unusually well-balanced and harmonious design for this area of the country. The
same architect marked out a completely new ground-plan of the main floor, which
included a music room with ceilings decorated with *trompe-l'oeil* paintings
representing the Arts and Sciences, together with portraits of members of the
Zurita family. The house has two gardens: the old one designed in 1630 on
two levels and the new one, recently laid out on the site of the former orchard
and vegetable garden.

The house of Domecq de la Riva is another lovely Jerez palace. It was
built at the end of the fifteenth century on a plot granted by Queen Isabel to Don
Esteban de Villacreces. The building guild (*Cabildo*) wrote to the Queen during its construction, complaining that a forbidden fortress house was being built.

Left CASA DE CAMPO REAL The Music Room was designed by the architect Juan de Vargas between 1785 and 1792. Its *trompe l'oeil* ceiling is painted to imitate plasterwork. The sepia allegories of the Arts and Sciences were devised in order not to distract guests during concerts.

CASA DE CAMPO REAL The little chamber next to the main bedroom has floral fabric covering the walls, a lovely set of chairs with their original tapestry covers and a nineteenth-century Venetian mirror.

CASA DE CAMPO REAL A string of
interlinking rooms ends with the
Music Room, seen here through the
open doorway.

CASA DE CAMPO REAL Two cosy
living rooms give onto a dining
room beyond.

CASA DE CAMPO REAL The main bedroom, with a sixteenth-century, velvet-covered clothes chest at the foot of the canopied bed and seventeenth-century, Spanish baroque stools either side. The *Temptation of St. Jerome* above the fireplace is attributed to Titian.

CASA DE CAMPO REAL The loggia arcade leading to the old garden has a *trompe l'oeil* ceiling painted as the sky.

Esteban de Villacreces was a controversial character; it appears, for example, that his ships practised piracy in the straight and captured Arabs and Christians indiscriminately. He was brother-in-law to Enrique IV's *Válido* (prime minister), Don Beltrán de la Cueva, and participated in the civil wars against the Duke of Medina Sidonia and later with the Catholic Sovereigns in the campaigns against Portugal and in the conquest of Granada. His plot of building land was a reward for these exploits.

During the war of Independence, the French plundered and almost destroyed the building. In the twentieth century, the house was bought and restored by the Domecq family. Its staircase and courtyard are of particular interest, as are the small oratory and the dining room, which contains sets of chinaware from the Indies.

PUERTO DE SANTA MARÍA

Not far from Jerez is Puerto de Santa María, the so-called city of a hundred palaces, which – in spite of the two towns being neighbours – are architecturally quite different from the Jerez mansions. In Santa María, the houses are more introspective. They do have courtyards, but only as passages with access to the various living areas. The storerooms or cellars *(bodegas)* are usually situated off the courtyard, as they are in the Casa de los Arcohermoso and the Casa de los Osborne, and all

CASA DE LOS DOMECQ DE LA RIVA   The dining room, with three rectangular, walnut-top tables and walnut and leather chairs. The walls are covered with a golden yellow fabric and exhibit a collection of chinaware. The skirting and door and window cases are marble.

CASA DE LOS DOMECQ DE LA RIVA   A bronze sculpture of a well-dressed woman on horseback.

Left CASA DE LOS DOMECQ DE LA RIVA The gallery, with an oratory at the back, its doors painted with unusual panels of stylized flowers, is dedicated to the Virgin of the Rosary.

Opposite CASA DE LOS DOMECQ DE LA RIVA A detail of the lavish oratory, showing an enthroned Christ.

Below CASA DE LOS DOMECQ DE LA RIVA The more sombre drawing room is hung with a large tapestry describing a battle scene.

Opposite QUINTA DE LOS TERRY, PUERTO DE SANTA MARÍA The exotic upper garden, with species hundreds of years old, was originally planted with specimens brought from the Americas.

of the houses were built with watch-towers, as many of their owners traded with the West Indies and their ships arrived at the port loaded with goods from the Americas.

This West Indian wealth is evident in the rich interiors of the houses, full of furniture made from exotic woods and paintings of American, Cuzqueño or Mexican origin. The most important areas of these mansions were nevertheless the gardens, which were planted with botanical specimens, often grown in an environment acclimatized for species brought from the Americas.

Quinta de los Terry is the house belonging to this family of long-standing wine producers and horse breeders. They arrived from Ireland, as many others, fleeing the wars of religion that raged at the end of the seventeenth century. At that time, Puerto was the site of the Capitanía General del Mar Océano, of which the Duke of Medinaceli was the highest authority; there was a constant movement of ships and goods and many of the town's inhabitants were wholesale traders with the West Indies and with foreign merchants. The Terry family settled here and built this house, which is surrounded by gardens and by an orchard, all of which have remained unaltered.

The one-storey house has a stone façade and a watch-tower, a central courtyard paved with white and black marble and a glass-covered loggia around it to let the light into the sitting rooms and bedrooms. It also possesses a lovely oratory with Cuzqueño images and an eighteenth-century coffered ceiling. Its gallery now exhibits a splendid collection of eighteenth-century Spanish and Italian writing-desks. Paintings by Murillo, Flemish paintings on wood and a portrait of Joseph Bonaparte from the school of Goya hang on the walls. The vast dining hall is soberly furnished, with two glass cabinets exhibiting a beautiful Cantonese china set. The whole long side of the gallery is glazed as a window looking over the terrace.

The garden is based on the design of an old botanical garden and occupies two levels: the lower, French-style one for winter and the shady, upper one for summer. Very old species like *jacarandas*, *araucarias* and Brazil nuts are grown there, as the garden was prepared to accommodate species arriving from the Americas.

Right in the town centre is the Casa de los Arcohermoso, originally an eighteenth-century *casa de labor* (workhouse), whose main features have survived. The living-quarters, as usual, were on the upper floor, the rest of the building being reserved for administrative areas, storerooms, cellars and stables.

The façade is of carved stone and the floors are paved with Tarifa tiles. A large part of the façade was once limewashed as a defence against epidemics – a very common measure at that time in view of the possibility of plague – but during the latest restoration works, the original stone was exposed.

The front door opens onto a lovely, landscaped, corner courtyard with a beautiful marble fountain; depressed moulded arches appear on two sides and blind walls on the other two. This type of courtyard, where the buildings adjoining the palace were adapted as storerooms, was very common in the town.

QUINTA DE LOS TERRY The chapel bell gable and ceramic and clay roof tiles, high above the gardens.

Left QUINTA DE LOS TERRY An interesting shadow is cast onto the carved wooden doors of the loggia.

Below QUINTA DE LOS TERRY The traditional and cosy living room, with family portraits and religious paintings.

QUINTA DE LOS TERRY A day-bed in a bedroom chamber, with a twentieth-century portrait by Hernan Cortés over the fireplace.

QUINTA DE LOS TERRY A black madonna from the New World is the centrepiece of the chapel's altar.

An eighteenth-century staircase, with a carved wood hand-rail, rises from one side of the courtyard. The courtyard itself leads onto a series of gardens at the rear, one of which is of Arab design.

The Osborne family house dates from the same period and has a similar structure. It also has a watch-tower, like those of buildings in Cadiz, because its original owners were probably traders with the West Indies. The courtyard and stairs now display an interesting array of hunting trophies.

ANTEQUERA

Because of an increase in agriculture, trade and craftmanship during the eighteenth century, building activity intensified in the small town of Antequera in the province of Malaga. Among the many mansions erected at that time, the Casa de las Columnas stands out as a result of its remarkable pink columns on the entrance arch. It was built in 1714 by the Marquis of Villadarias on his return from America. He brought with him a Virgin of Guadalupe, painted by Juan Correa, which he installed on the wall of the staircase and had framed with

Opposite QUINTA DE LOS TERRY The loggia, with its religious paintings and icons.

QUINTA DE LOS TERRY The great dining room is furnished with an English table and cane-seated chairs.

Above CASA DE ARCOHERMOSO, PUERTO DE SANTA MARÍA The courtyard leads to the garden and to other secondary courtyards – the comfortable gallery of one of which is seen here – which were originally storehouses, cellars and other annexes.

Left CASA DE ARCOHERMOSO The 'Piano Room', furnished with a range of chairs.

Opposite CASA DE ARCOHERMOSO A view of the covered gallery leading onto the garden, with its collection of Spanish earthenware.

Opposite CASA DE ARCOHERMOSO The prettily furnished and sunny upper-floor loggia.

Left CASA DE ARCOHERMOSO The dining room is furnished in English style, but the carpet was made in the Real Fábrica. The large painting is a copy of a work by Jacopo Bassano (1517–92).

CASA DE ARCOHERMOSO A portrait of a composed Spanish lady with a fan, on the wall above an oak chest.

CASA DE OSBORNE, PUERTO DE SANTA MARÍA
A rather terrifying array of hunting trophies is on display on the walls of the staircase.

Opposite CASA DE LAS COLUMNAS The courtyard's red stone columns, after which the house is named, harmonize subtly with the lichen-covered stone flags.

CASA DE LAS COLUMNAS Close-up of the glorious red stone of the columns, echoed at the foot of the staircase.

plasterwork. The courtyard and stairs were originally decorated with frescos, but they were covered with limewash after the plague epidemic.

Felipe V visited the house and had to stay for several days, because his son fell ill. This unexpected sojourn earned the owners a number of privileges, one of which was the right to exhibit carved chains on the doorway as proof that a king had been a guest in the house. At the end of the century, the Marquis sold the mansion to the Blázquez de Lora family, who still live in it.

The doorway, from which the palace derives its name, is flanked by two pairs of pink marble columns rising from a base and has a balcony resting on the lintel. The area behind the door is a *casapuerta*, with a covered *apeadero* leading in an unusual way directly to the main courtyard. The courtyard, smaller and more secluded than those seen in Écija, is surrounded by a single loggia, also with pink marble columns. From the *casapuerta* rises a splendid stone staircase, with beautifully preserved panels of Granada tiles and a ceiling with magnificent plasterwork, also from Granada, by the Brueño brothers.

Opposite CASA DE LAS COLUMNAS The floor tiles are equally dramatic on this floor of the house: terracotta interwoven with polychrome ceramic.

CASA DE LAS COLUMNAS The living room has dramatic diamond and zig-zag tiled skirting.

MODERN TIMES

DURING THE NINETEENTH CENTURY, a few interesting palaces were still being built in Andalusia: the colonial-style house known as Carmen de los Mártires; the more French-style Palacio de Torres Cabrera in Cordoba; the colonial Hotel Colón in Huelva; and the eclectic Isabelline palace of Moreno-Mora in Cadiz. But none of these buildings can be categorized under a specific architectural classification, and far less can they be considered to belong to a typically Andalusian style.

There are several possible reasons for this architectural laxity. The first is economic: power and money had by then moved to other, more solid, regions of the country, where great houses were built during the second half of the nineteenth century for an increasingly wealthy and powerful middle class. They were designed according to the latest fashions: modernist in Barcelona, colonial in Asturias, Isabelline and French in Madrid, for example.

Another reason for the decline of an Andalusian style of building was that during the nineteenth century, energetic young architects appeared on the scene with extensive knowledge of building elsewhere in Europe and in America. Their proposals were therefore not regionalist, but international. Moreover, the new town-planning projects developed at the time included the construction of large, rational, middle-class buildings for several families, rather than grand private houses.

The manor houses that were built in Andalusia also followed the prevailing, eclectic fashion that mixed the best of each style – but here it was used with a difference. The old tradition of genuine Arab art, based on the teachings of the *ulemas* of Granada, for which the Moorish palaces were so famous, survived in spite of fashion and the passing of time.

Page 206 PALACIO DE TORRES CABRERA, CORDOBA The open and airy courtyard, which has a glazed loggia. The fragments of Roman mosaics set in at the top of the arches represent the Muses and the Seasons.

Right CARMEN DE LOS MÁRTIRES, GRANADA The arches of the loggia around the building were inspired by those of the Alhambra.

Opposite CARMEN DE LOS MÁRTIRES The garden of the house, designed in the French style.

CARMEN DE LOS MÁRTIRES The grotto, with its pretty nymph fountain.

The palace of Torres Cabrera in Cordoba dates from the last third of the nineteenth century and belongs today to the Cruz Conde family. It has a different structure to the houses of earlier centuries. A wrought-iron gate opens onto a magnificent, landscaped courtyard. The building is a *palacete* of neo-classical design, reminiscent of French palaces. To right and left, the two wings of the palace advance towards the circular railing. One of them was the coach house, now displaying some magnificent carriages, and the other housed the stables. The central section of the building is formed by two floors, with a striking portico of white marble columns holding up a balcony with an iron balustrade.

Left CARMEN DE LOS MÁRTIRES The glazed-in access courtyard to the house. It has a modern, minimal feel, with plain fluted pilasters.

CARMEN DE LOS MÁRTIRES A living room on the upper floor; Morcillo's painting *The Spinners* hangs between the windows.

PALACIO DE TORRES CABRERA The rather grand staircase has marble balustrades and steps, stucco walls and a medieval bride's chest on the landing.

Opposite PALACIO DE TORRES CABRERA A small, informal dining room with geometric tiled floor.

Abundant coats-of-arms of the Fernández de Cordoba and the Martel families are displayed on the upper part of the building and bear the date 1867, the year of its completion.

Through the main entrance and three more iron gates is the lovely and very unusual courtyard. The smaller yard on the left contains a wonderful, second-century Roman mosaic depicting the head of Bacchus. The courtyard has a single, now glass-covered, loggia with white marble columns. The arcade holds up the covered upper galleries. The arch spandrels contain fragments of Roman mosaics illustrating the Seasons and the Senses that were discovered at the same time as the Bacchus mosaic. From one side of the courtyard rises a sumptuous staircase, paved with black marble and with stucco walls.

Before the upper floor was completed, the ballroom – one of its most brilliant rooms – was opened. The Duke and Duchess of Montpensier attended the ceremony, which was presided over by Alfonso XII, who was visiting Cordoba.

The room measures fifteen metres by six and contains gold and red Louis XV furniture, as well as collections of Retiro and Sèvres china and a lovely, white marble fireplace. The present construction of the Carmen de los Mártires dates from the nineteenth century, although its origin goes back far further. The palace was restored in the 1980s.

The *cármenes* of Granada are small properties built on the slopes of the Albaicín near the Alhambra (in the same way as the Gigarrales of Toledo), looking down over the city and the fertile plain Their name derives from the Arabic *karm*, meaning vineyard. They are really garden houses, surrounded by high limewashed walls for privacy and facing the valley of Granada. Chronicles recount how around 1448, before the *Conquista*, the foothills of the Albaicín were covered with these little properties. Most of the *cármenes* that have survived date from the seventeenth and eighteenth centuries, although their origins are much earlier. These buildings were thought to be of Christian design, but the Arab influence on their architecture and landscaping is plain. In fact, after the Conquest, the Christians took advantage of and adapted the existing buildings to their needs, as they had done elsewhere.

The steeply sloped terrain made it necessary to follow certain standards in the lay-outs and ground-plans of both houses and gardens. As in almost all Andalusian houses, the rooms were situated on the ground floor, although here they opened directly onto the gardens. These were the real jewels of the *cármenes*. They were genuine, landscaped orchards, with terraces and pergolas forming separate open-air 'rooms' where flowers and aromatic plants like rosemary, lavender and *santolina* blended harmoniously with vegetables and with myrtle and cypress trees. Bowers, covered galleries and turrets offered secluded corners for enjoying the park in total privacy.

The gardens were steeply terraced, with steps, walls of large fruit trees, climbing plants and enormous cypresses between each level. Following the Koranic tradition of not exhibiting signs of the household's wealth and importance to the outside, the *cármenes* were surrounded by high walls. Access to a house was through an independent ante-garden, guaranteeing privacy. On the ground floor were reception rooms and rooms opening onto the garden and the courtyard, with shady galleries. There was often an attic on the top floor with a watch-tower above it. Water was, of course, essential in Arab gardens. Its sound was celestial music and its constant flowing from the tank along the little canals to the fountains helped refresh the air during the long hot summers.

PALACIO DE TORRES CABRERA An octagonal Roman mosaic head of Bacchus is displayed on the wall of the carriage entrance above a contemporary portrait bust.

The Carmen de los Mártires is a property occupying about seventeen acres on a southern slope below the walls of the Alhambra. It is said that it was here, on 4 April 1492, that a defeated and disconsolate Boabdil, the last of the Nasrid kings, handed the keys of the city to Cardinal Mendoza, representative of Ferdinand and Isabel. To commemorate the event, Queen Isabel ordered a chapel to be built, dedicated to the Holy Martyrs, in memory of the Christians who had suffered martyrdom and imprisonment during the Arab domination.

Later, the chapel passed to the order of the Barefooted Carmelites, of which the poet and saint, Juan de la Cruz, was prior for six years, from 1582 to 1588. The garden contains a luxuriant cedar planted by the saint and to which he refers in his *Noche Oscura*. The crenellations of the Alhambra palace can be seen clearly from the garden.

During the French occupation, the chapel was converted into a barn, and after Mendizabal's loss of entailment to the lands in 1845, the palace had several private owners, until it was bought by the Duke of the Infantado in the 1930s. During all that time, the house and gardens were modified, destroyed, reconstructed and neglected. The present building is a four-storey neo-classic *palacete*, one of the best examples of mid-nineteenth century Spanish architecture. Again, it is designed according to the prevailing eclectic style, with abundant details inspired by early industrial developments, combined with classical motifs.

Under the care of the Infantado family, the *cármen* recovered its past splendour; the gardens were embellished and a new life given to the house, to such an extent that the property was declared of artistic interest in 1943. But after it became municipal property, a series of alterations almost ruined it completely, until the house was properly restored and the gardens reconstructed in the 1980s. They are now open to the public in the city of Granada.

Twentieth-century examples of Sevillian manor house architecture include the buildings constructed for a 1929 exhibition of architecture and design. Several of them, built by the architect Anibal González, were originally intended as pavilions for the various countries participating in the exhibition, although today most of them are in private hands.

Around 1940, an unusual house was built in the Paseo de la Palmera. Designed by the architect Felipe Medina, it was a whim of its proprietress, a woman from Malaga who wanted to live near the city centre, but in a modern house. Built on what had been the Santa Elena market gardens, the striking features of the house are its elevations and shape, designed to take maximum advantage of the sunlight and to open onto the grand garden. The glass-covered, curved loggias on the ground floor give it a rather English appearance. When its present owners bought it over ten years ago, they modernized and restored the basic utilities, whilst respecting the spirit in which this original house was conceived.

Opposite CASA DE LOS MARQUESES DE MÉRITO,
SEVILLE The comfortable, inner, curved loggia.
The paintings on the walls are Sevillian and
the flowered upholstery is Cretonne.

CASA DE LOS MARQUESES DE MÉRITO
The 'Piano Room', with a large still-life of
flowers and, on the right, three French
mirrors.

Here we end our walk though this vast region of Spain, which has so attracted travellers' attention throughout the centuries. We have stopped at many manor houses – but not all – in different places, dating from various periods and featuring a range of styles and influences. We have witnessed the difficulties that are involved in the preservation over almost five centuries of a national patrimony held in private hands. We have seen both the similarities and the contrasts between the buildings and, above all, we have been struck by the forethought of the owners who, by conserving these treasures, have kept alive their love for Andalusia.

Andalusia is a magical place, where almost everything is Islamic in origin. Its fairytale palaces attempt to capture fragrances and colours in their lovely, dream-like gardens and courtyards. The colours of the flowers and of the marbles, of the natural, whitish paint and the limewash, the perfumes of orange blossom and myrtle and jasmine, all stay in our imagination. The sound of water trickling along little canals or flowing from spouts, of birdsong, of a candle spluttering out, or of guitar music coming from the depths of a palace, remain with us. We have seen a world of traditions and of ancestral customs blended in villages and towns: this is the land of vivid language, of the *cante jondo* and gay street life, of bullfighters and *bandoleros*, of the Álvarez Quinteros and Juan Ramón Jiménez, of Falla and Garcia Lorca, of Bécquer and the Machados, of Alberti and Curro Romero.

And if you wander through the narrow streets at siesta time anywhere in Andalusia and peep through an iron lattice gate, the half light, the whisper of a fountain and the perfume of orange blossom will be stamped on your memory forever.

CASA DE LOS MARQUESES DE MÉRITO The back of the house is gently curved, with large windows and a door opening onto the rear gardens.

Opposite CASA DE LOS MARQUESES DE MÉRITO A corner of the chapel, with its fifteenth-century monstrance. A collection of rosaries hangs from the wall. The ceiling is painted blue and decorated with stars.

BIBLIOGRAPHY

Angulo Iñiguez, D., *Arquitectura Mudéjar Sevillana de los Siglos XIII, XIV y XV*, Seville, 1983

Cervera Vera, Luis, *Historia de la Arquitectura Española*, Planeta, Madrid

Lamperez y Romea, V., *Arquitectura Civil Espatura Española de los Siglos XIII, X* , Madrid, 1993

Galera, P., *La Arquitectura después de Vandelvira*, Madrid, 1992

Gonzalez Cordón, A., *Sevilla, Vivienda y Ciudad, 1848/1929*, Seville, 1985

Manjon Mergerina, R., *Palacio de Lebrija*, Seville, 1970

Mena, J.M., *Leyendas y Tradiciones Sevillanas*, Plaza & Janes, 1996

Palacios, J., *La Cantería en la Construcción del Renacimiento Andaluz*, Madrid, 1992

Sanchez Corbacho, A., *Arquitectura Barroca Sevillana en el Siglo XVIII*, Madrid, 1984

Sanchez Trigueros, J.A., *Palacios de Espasña*, Espasa-Calpe, Madrid

Schezen, Roberto and Junquera, Juan Luis, *Spanish Splendor*, New York, 1992

Various authors, *Arte y Arquitectura en la Vivienda Española*, Cinterco, F.c.c., 1996

Various authors, *Casas y Palacios de Al – Andalus (s. XII y XIII)*, Sierra Nevada, 1995

Various authors, *La Arquitectura del Renacimiento en Andalucía*, Seville, 1992

Washington, Irving, *Cuentos de la Alhambra*, Cátedra, 1996

ÍNDEX

Page numbers in *italic* refer to captions to
illustrations.
Page numbers in **bold** type indicate main
references to a subject.